Rebekah and I have been friends for years. I've always been impressed with both the clarity of her message and the vulnerability and courage with which she delivers it. This book is no exception. It's not the story of her life, it's about what she's learned watching Jesus invade her life. She doesn't tell you what to do; she talks about who to trust.

BOB GOFF, author of *Love Does*

We consider Rebekah and Gabe to be a Godsend in our lives. Many times after sharing a warm-hearted meal, we leave inspired to take yet another step and deeper stride into our own stories of freedom. In reading Rebekah's gracious and honest words, you will be inspired to take your own steps with him in freedom. May you find the sweet space where he tends to your heart, bringing life to places you can't currently fathom. May he surprise you with each turn of the page.

CHRIS AND LAUREN TOMLIN, songwriter and worship leader

You Are Free sent me to my knees pleading with God to show me where I have missed the freedom he intended for me. It opened my eyes to places I was holding on to self, to doubt, to worry, and sent me in search of more intimacy and a deeper, fuller trust in him. Rebekah tells the truth about her journey as a child of God; a wife, mother, daughter, and friend. She invites us to a place where full reliance on him is the only way to truly be free.

KORIE ROBERTSON, *Duck Dynasty*

When we first met Rebekah, we felt known and loved immediately. That's what reading *You Are Free* is like. Rebekah invites you to peek into her journey as she finds freedom in Christ and invites us to do the same. This book is an anthem for healing, freedom, and hope in your life.

JEFF AND ALYSSA BETHKE, authors of *Jesus > Religion* and *Spoken For*

Rebekah is a sister who fights for the freedom of others. We talked in the early stages of her dreaming about this message and I told her, "You have to write this." The anthem of freedom isn't for a distant future, but for here and now. This book declares, as long as there is a beat in our heart, we are called to be free.

CHRISTINE CAINE,

The first time I met Rebekah, I left feeling nearer to Jesus, because I knew her intimacy with him could not be staged or put on. This book won't leave you with a to-do list or an ache in your soul to improve, but simply an invitation from someone who lives free. You'll be drawn to the foot of the cross, to worship outside the empty grave, and to embrace your freedom and the freedom of others.

JESS CONNOLLY, founder of the Influence Network and
Amen Paper Company and author of *Wild and Free*

I wasn't but a few pages in and wanted to shout for joy because of the power of this message. Rebekah opens up her life with refreshing authenticity and a deep commitment to Scripture. She brilliantly points out that true freedom is found when God is enough in our lives and when he has become our all. *You Are Free* is a call for every believer to experience the strength of God in our weakness, the beauty of God in our ashes, and the confidence of God in our insecurities.

BANNING LIEBSCHER, Jesus Culture founder and pastor

My favorite teachers teach from the trenches. Rebekah has done the work and fought for her own freedom and now is fighting for ours. I have seen my friend cry tears for your freedom. Prepare to enjoy being fought for by God through these words.

JENNIE ALLEN, founder and visionary,
IF:Gathering and author of *Nothing to Prove*

The freedom to be exactly who God created is something we all search for. With hope, beauty, and the expertise of a skillful guide, Rebekah takes us on a journey back to living each day in the joy of being our truest self. A truly remarkable book!

MIKE FOSTER, author of *People of the Second Chance:
A Guide to Bringing Life-Saving Love to the World*

Scripture boldly declares, "It is for freedom that Christ has set us free," and yet many of us cannot hear clearly, let alone enter into this truth amid the clutter of our distractions, anxieties, sorrows, fatigue, regrets, loneliness, shame, and other freedom-inhibiting realities. After reading this book in a single sitting, I felt more known, more forgiven, more loved, and more hopeful in Jesus.

SCOTT SAULS, pastor of Christ Presbyterian Church in Nashville, Tennessee, and author of *Jesus Outside the Lines* and *Befriend*

Rebekah displays freedom with candor, vulnerability, and truth; laying her heart bare on the page. If followers of Christ learned to speak, teach, live, and exude this freedom, I believe heaven would bend to earth in a way that we have yet to see.

ADAM AND DAWNTOYA THOMASON, historian and cultural anthropologists

You Are Free is an extraordinary book, a wonderful mix of heart, vulnerability, practical advice, and personal stories. Rebekah leaves you feeling like a friend who sat at the same table, asked the same questions, and found permission to truly be free.

HAVILAH CUNNINGTON, director of Moral Revolution and founder of Truth to Table

YOU ARE FREE

BE WHO YOU ALREADY ARE

REBEKAH LYONS

Foreword by ANN VOSKAMP

ZONDERVAN BOOKS

ZONDERVAN BOOKS

You Are Free
Copyright © 2017 by Rebekah Lyons

Published in Grand Rapids, Michigan, by Zondervan. Zondervan is a registered trademark of The Zondervan Corporation, L.L.C., a wholly owned subsidiary of HarperCollins Christian Publishing, Inc.

Requests for information should be addressed to customercare@harpercollins.com.

Zondervan titles may be purchased in bulk for educational, business, fundraising, or sales promotional use. For information, please email SpecialMarkets@Zondervan.com.

ISBN 978-0-310-36938-7 (softcover)
ISBN 978-0-310-35026-2 (audio)
ISBN 978-0-310-34556-5 (ebook)

Author is represented by Christopher Ferebee, Attorney and Literary Agent, www.christopher ferebee.com.

Cover design: Curt Diepenhorst
Cover illustration: Dana Tanamachi
Interior design: Kait Lamphere

Printed in the United States of America

HB 03.06.2024

For Cade, Pierce, and Kennedy;
May you remain as free as you are today,
where Jesus is only a whisper away.

Christ has set us free to live a free life.
So take your stand!
Never again let anyone put a
harness of slavery on you.
Just make sure that you don't use this
freedom as an excuse to do whatever you
want to do and destroy your freedom.
Rather, use your freedom to serve
one another in love;
that's how freedom grows.
For everything we know about God's
Word is summed up in a single sentence:
Love others as you love yourself.
That's an act of true freedom.
If you bite and ravage each other, watch out—
in no time at all you will be annihilating
each other, and where will your
precious freedom be then?
Live freely,
animated and motivated by God's Spirit.

GALATIANS 5:1, 13–16 MSG

Contents

Foreword

M Y GRANDAD TOLD ME a story once and that story became a light.

A light that unlocks the dark and releases you into the land of a thousand suns.

Apparently, so the story went, there had been a tropical snake, longer than the length of a man, that wound its way up the stilts of a jungle cabana and slithered right into one unsuspecting woman's kitchen.

That woman turned around, split the day with one blood-curdling scream, and flung herself outside wide-eyed. That's about when a machete-wielding neighbor showed up, calmly walked into her kitchen, and sliced off the head of the reptilian thing.

The strange thing is that a snake's neurology and blood flow make it such that a snake still slithers wild even after it's been sliced headless.

For hours that woman stood outside, waiting.

And the body of the snake still rampaged on, thrashing hard against windows and walls, destroying chairs and table and all things good and home.

My Grandad turned to say it, and I can tell you, it felt like a proclamation of emancipation:

A snake can only wreak havoc until it accepts it has no head—*that it's actually dead.*

The enemy of your soul can only wreak havoc in your life until you accept that it's already dead—and you're already free.

Be who you already are.

Be Free — because you already are free.

Your enemy is dead — so silence the lies in your head.

No enemy can't imprison you — because your Savior empowers you.

Nothing can hold you in bondage — because you are held by him.

Not one thing can hold you back — because his arms are holding you.

"Christ doesn't say you can be or may be or will be free. He says you are free," Rebekah's words flame right here in these pages that are about to become a light, a key, in your very own hands.

I spent more than a month with Rebekah during the year this

book, these words, grew like a flame in her heart. Together, we poured over Scripture in a kibbutz outside of Jerusalem; literally walked the Emmaus road under stars; and prayed for our hearts to burn within us, that we might recognize Christ whatever road he had us on; stood under an arching double rainbow in Colorado and boldly trusted God for all of his promises; got down on our knees, our faces, broke our hearts before the heart of God under a Rocky Mountain rain. What you hold in your hands isn't an idea—it's an incarnation. Rebekah has enfleshed this freedom and I've witnessed it firsthand: Rebekah's freefall to fly has transformed her into a blazing harbinger of desperately needed reality: *Be who you already are.*

Is there a message that your soul needs more?

The greatest lie of the pit is that you have to prove yourself.

This is the lie that's bound you and ripped your heart out in a million ways.

The greatest truth of Christ's reality is that you are free — so live free. *Be who you already are.*

The snake's dead—*so silence the lies in your head.*

And the glory of true freedom is?

You are always made free *from* something — to become free *for* something.

This is what the realest love does — it frees you *from* slavery and frees you *for* serving. From slavery to the dark to serving in the kingdom of light! From slavery to meaningless pain—to serving for the most meaningful purpose.

Bind yourself to Christ and you are free from everything else that binds.

Love always asks you to give up some freedoms to get the greatest freedoms of all: Security. Safety. Intimacy.

Freedom is not about doing whatever we want most—but the opportunity to do what is *most Christlike.*

Freedom is not having any limitations—freedom is having the best limitations for life transformation and realizations and destinations.

Hold these pages like a burning flame in the palm of your hands, like a begging, blazing key, like a bit of glowing sun that will grow you into freedom soaring on wind.

The snake is still. *Your saving is here.*

"God never guides us at some time in the future, but always here and now.

Realize that the Lord is here now, and the freedom you receive is immediate," wrote Oswald Chambers. Rebekah echoes these words.

You Are Free

Immediate freedom.

Begin.

You are released.

ANN VOSKAMP,
author of the *New York Times* bestsellers
The Broken Way & *One Thousand Gifts*

Introduction

J STARTED WRITING this freedom story two years ago. I felt confident and full of faith as I began to walk it out, with almost a sense of bravado about the idea of God's goodness. I wanted to shout from the rooftops, "Let's all get free so we can get about the work!" Easy-peasy, right?

But when the time for writing came, the words dried up. Perhaps I hadn't quite cracked the code on freedom after all. *If God wants to set captives free*, I thought, *then let's do this already*. We simply need to release our grip on the bars and step out of our metaphorical jail cells into this abundant life, right? And yet the minute I tried to articulate this truth in written form, I felt more enslaved than ever before.

The dry spell sent me reeling. I said to God, "I can't do this! I'm ill-equipped." If I really believed this freedom thing, it would mean Jesus was enough to free me from *anything*, any kind of brokenness I carried in this world. Although I'd experienced a taste of the freedom God has for me, the darkness in our world still felt too great.

I thought, *Maybe full freedom is just something we hope for and stay*

*quiet about, not to be realized until heaven. Maybe I'm crazy to write
a book about it.*

I went back to the pages of Scripture, which assured me that we are
to live as people who are free[1] because Christ has already set us free,[2]
and gave us the Spirit to keep us free.[3] Furthermore, Jesus declared
a kingdom come—a kingdom of complete freedom—here on earth
as it is in heaven,[4] and Paul teaches that this kingdom power lives
in us.[5] This means that even in our feeble weakness, if we claim
Christ and his resurrection, somehow we are God's agents who carry
freedom to the world.

Why don't we see this kind of kingdom-come freedom more? What
Scripture teaches about freedom and what we witness in our everyday
lives are two opposing realities. We hobble through our days, yet we
long for the God of the grand gesture, the one who splits the seas
where they surface and exposes the foundations of the world with a
single breath.[6] Jesus promised life abundant, but this challenges our
experience of brokenness and captivity. How often do we wonder,
Is what the Bible teaches true?

We want the Jesus who beckons us out on the water, the Jesus who
takes our feeble offering, blesses it, and multiplies it. And yet, here we
are, living our lives one small step at a time, feeling so powerless to
loosen the chains that bind us, let alone help others live in freedom.

We can know in our minds that God has set us free—when we were young we may have even learned and memorized verses telling us this—and *still* God's power has not rescued us from the pit. The good news is that sometimes God uses the pit to teach us about freedom. In the pit, we become aware of our captivity; we can no longer deny we are enslaved. When we are in the pit, there is no mistaking our bondage.

Galatians is the book on freedom, and it's not written to those outside the church, it's written to the church. Paul saw the temptation of the religious to add works to the story of Jesus' death and resurrection (rendering the cross not enough). He reacted strongly to this for six chapters, making sure we understand when Christ calls us to a free life, he calls us to operate out of the freedom *he has already given us.*

This is the point of good news, the gospel. We cannot add to it, or diminish it. Paul urges, "It is for freedom that Christ has set us free. Stand firm, then, and do not let yourselves be burdened again by a yoke of slavery."[7]

Paul's poignant words echo in our hallowed halls today.

How many of us have lost our way? Maybe we knew freedom in grade school, in college, or in our early twenties, but somewhere along the way our freedom turned to survival, and we put on masks too painful to take off. We began to condemn ourselves with our own words, saying, "We are too much," or "We are too little." Yet God persisted.

Freedom comes when we know God is enough, when he is our every-thing. When he is our peace and our strength, joy, and rest. Our provision, healer, hope, fortress, shelter, strong tower, and Father. Freedom reveals everything good is from him and by him and for him. Every breath we take, every person we encounter, every word we utter is all an expression of a freedom where God dwells in us and loves through us!

What if we became this kind of dwelling place? Where we allowed him to set us free, so we could help set others free?

In the upcoming pages I will walk you through my own journey into this kind of freedom so that you might begin to grow in freedom too. I suspect we will laugh and cry a bit, if my writing process gives any indication. We will wrestle through tough realities. I'll ask questions, some easy to answer and others painful to recount. My only request is that you leave nothing on the table. No stone unturned, no whispers unspoken, no secret still hidden. This freedom thing is costly but *worth it*.

Freedom is for everyone who wants it—the lost, the wounded, and those weary from all of the striving. It's for those who gave up trying years ago. It's for professional Christians hiding secrets. It's for the angry and hurt, for those both brilliant and burnt by the Christian song and dance. I write for you, for all of you. You are the church, the people of God. You were meant to be free.

Will you join in this freedom journey with me?

1

To Be
Free

*Tell the truth and write about freedom
and fight for it, however you can,
and you will be richly rewarded.*
ANNE LAMOTT[1]

ALL MY LIFE I've run the hamster wheel of achievement and acceptance; a headstrong, Type-A control freak, looking for love. As a child I earned love by working hard to fit in. At church I earned love by memorizing verses. At school I earned love by pleasing teachers. Looking back, I see a girl in pigtails, acceptance her end game. In kindergarten, I repeated the sinner's prayer before I could write complete sentences, the fear of eternal fire motivation enough. I memorized King James verses with words like *sanctification, edification,* and *fornication.* I regurgitated the definition of *justification*—"just-as-if-I-hadn't-sinned"—even though I didn't understand what the words meant. I absorbed all this burdensome religion like a six-, seven-, and eight-year-old sponge, and furthermore, I believed it must be true, all of it.

Religion reigned.

In school, I served on the patrol squad, an honor given to the eldest and wisest of Elementaryland. I pinned a silver safety badge to my orange plastic vest and shoved the matching orange hard hat over my blonde curls, my chest puffed out with pride. (This began my affection for hats; I'm sure of it!) Taking very seriously our directive to enforce the school rules, I and the rest of the patrol squad would count to five as each subordinate took his or her turn at the water fountain. We carried the great responsibility of opening and closing car doors at pickup, impressing parents with the safety of their fledglings, encouraging them with our *Have-a-nice-days*.

Responsibility reigned.

Around that time, I picked up the trumpet. I wanted to play flute or clarinet like my girlfriends in elementary band, but my older brother was already renting a trumpet as a sophomore in high school. My parents informed me that if I wanted to play an instrument, I would have to share his. There was no financial margin for two rentals. And so, I picked up that shiny brass instrument, and standing in front of my mama's full-length bedroom mirror, I blew my heart out, squawking like a dying blue heron. Would I ever make that thing sing?

The trumpet became my ticket to being *somebody*, to being relevant or important. By seventh grade I attended band camp in North Carolina and played "How Great Thou Art" solo in front of a few hundred kids. As a sophomore, I sat first chair in trumpet, ahead of thirteen boys. As a junior and senior, I marched my way into competitions around the country, earning trophies as the drum major for our high school marching band, the Royal Ambassadors.

Achievement reigned.

A good girl in church, I continued to memorize Bible verses, played my heart out on the trumpet in the church orchestra, and only cussed with the cool kids at the back of the fourth grade playground. A chameleon of sorts, I adjusted my behavior to align with my environment throughout my tweens, with popularity as my goal. By high school I could read any social situation from a mile away. I was voted onto the homecoming court each year. Being liked was top priority; it made me feel important.

Donning ballet flats or Doc Martens, singing along to Amy Grant or The Cure, dating football players or percussionists, I worked to fit in with whoever surrounded me: athletes, musicians, cheerleaders, honor society members, student government members, brainiacs, teachers' kids, and doctors' kids. I kept my cool, grasping for permission to be fully known, and in spite of that, fully loved. Whether as a student government officer, honor society member, or drum major of the marching band, I joined in the performing. It was addicting, but I was good at the game.

Popularity reigned.

I ran miles around my neighborhood my senior year in high school, trying to wrestle things out as my feet hit the pavement. Who was this God who created me, and for what purpose? I'd learned the ways of religion, responsibility, and achievement. I'd learned the ways of fitting in, of popularity, and of being liked. But what about freedom? The God I was striving for was rigid and lifeless and seemed far away. And although I believed he was real, I wasn't convinced he was good. So I went on trying to be the best version of myself, hoping maybe I'd catch a glimpse of his approval. Legalism shaped me, driving my performance as I sought to earn his love.

During my freshman year of college I gained fifteen pounds. After being mortified by how I looked in a Christmas family portrait, I worked hard to regain the ideal physical version of myself. I ratcheted up my running by spring, taking to the hills on a road behind campus we called "the roller coaster." Up and down and up and down I ran, the motion a metaphor for the way I felt inside. I waited tables at Applebee's, only allowing myself one French fry at the end of my eight-hour shift. If I ate a gummy bear, I followed it up with twenty jumping jacks to burn off the calories. My roomies worried, but the boys noticed. I liked the attention.

Approval reigned.

If someone had asked me in my youth, *Why all the striving?* I wouldn't have had an answer. It took decades to peel back the layers of bondage. At the time, I held relational intimacy at arm's length.

Come, but not too close; share, but not too much; live, but not too freely.

These were the mantras of my youth. I accepted the unspoken family, church, and social rule: *Keep up or suffer shame.* This message drove me to hustle for my worth at all costs. Quitting meant failure.

Strive to please; avoid shame; rinse and repeat.

Whenever I felt rejected or insecure, I buckled down with strategies to be more confident, more accepted, and more loved. I watched what others were doing and adopted their games. But the more I learned, the more fraudulent it all appeared. The cooler the person, the more fractured the heart.

Every now and then, someone I knew would be honest about their struggles, and I'd breathe a sigh of relief. Finally! Someone was admitting life was hard, giving me permission to do the same. But this glimpse of vulnerability was always fleeting and never took place from a stage, especially in church.

I read freedom in the pages of Scripture, but it felt elusive and temporary. I belted out the hymn "Victory in Jesus" loud and often, although I couldn't find tangible victory myself. God's truth never changed or went away; I simply couldn't hear it over the clamor of religion. I couldn't hear God's voice when my head was down, when I was pursuing my own agenda or working to please others. I wore myself ragged trying to be enough, and it wore me out. I longed to be free.

Many months ago, I walked a Florida beach at sunset, Gabe and the kids having already gone inside. I lingered on the shore like a rebellious teen, watching the last sliver of crimson sun slip under the waves, far out on the horizon. Streaky pinks and golds burned into my mind, unlocking my memory of rhythm. And there, on the beach, I danced.

In the twisting and twirling, I recalled similar moments from high school. I remembered dancing in our living room each morning after the rest of my family left for the day, Erasure's "A Little Respect" blaring in my ears. When the song was over, I'd collapse in dizziness, regrouping and racing my ten-speed bicycle to school, arriving just seconds before the bell. This routine preserved something true and necessary.

I remembered, too, elementary evenings when Mama called me in at dusk. I lingered even then, pumping the pedals of my bike in an even cadence as I rode alone with God in the secret place, away from all the striving. In those days, I felt the least alone and most accepted in the secret places. *These were the rare moments when I felt completely free.*

There, two decades later on a Florida beach, I found that rhythm again as I danced. I felt a glimpse of the freedom God longed for me to live into, a reckless abandon blooming into unencumbered joy. As the wind picked up under the cotton candy sky, I pictured the Almighty looking down, eyes landing on his little girl leaping on the beach. Spontaneous and awkward, though I didn't care, I embraced this déjà vu moment alone with him at dusk. *This is what freedom feels like. This is the way I was meant to live,* I thought.

What strikes me now is this: even before I walked into healing and freedom, I believed in the Christ who came to set me free. God, the author and perfecter of my faith, kept me believing that freedom was found in him, even when others around me gave up. Even when my friends, youth group acquaintances, and classmates walked away from faith, I still believed. Come to think of it, maybe it's a miracle I believed in the notion of freedom. God gave me faith, even in my bondage. He knew I was free in him, even if I didn't yet understand it.

Maybe this is the miracle of grace.

From the beginning of time, all God ever wanted was our union with him. He didn't create Adam and Eve because he wanted help cultivating the earth or naming the animals. Believe me, God is capable of this all by himself! No, he created man and woman because he wanted to offer companionship. They were the pinnacles of his creation. He delighted in Adam and Eve and wanted intimacy with them. His purpose for them—and us—was freedom to walk with him.

When I read the second chapter in Genesis, I picture Adam and Eve walking arm in arm with God across a wide meadow in the cool of the day. Eve throws her head back and laughs at their banter. The sun casts brilliant, yet soft light on the grain. The golden hour, they call it. The three of them walk around a bend and look out across a river, where the rays of sunlight dance. The wind rustles the grass for a moment, then stops. All is hushed and reverent.

The Eve of my imagination has made me a light-chaser all my life. In the golden hour, the Son feels close, as if he's kissing the earth. Perhaps that's why all of humanity craves a sunset. It's why I crave it.

Even now, when I take Communion in church, I feel the presence of my union with God. As I examine my heart, confessing my sin, eating his bread, and drinking from his cup, I receive the forgiveness of the new covenant. I'm reminded of God's closeness and my oneness with him. He takes my hand, as close as he was to Eve in the garden of Eden. He's always wanted garden walks and beachfront twirls with me, arm in arm. He wants them with you too. This is the God we serve, the one who calls us son or daughter, his beloved.

The freedom of Adam and Eve before the fall (even if it only lasted for a moment) is what makes captivity so heartbreaking. Consider the phrase in Hebrews, the "sin that so easily entangles."[2] Like a vapor, it seeps in and covers our heads, blocks us from seeing the truth that's been there all along—Christ has come to set us free! Sin creates confusion where what's right seems wrong and what's wrong seems right. Striving, rebellion, lack of faith, bitterness—all of these things keep us in bondage.

Until I began my journey toward freedom, the rules and regulations of legalism were weights that held me hostage. My desire for popularity, for relevance—this was bondage too. But most of all, *work* was my prison. I believed my value was only as good as my latest accomplishment. I never stopped hustling—there was always more worth to be earned. By this type of measuring stick, I'd never be enough. I chased life by the tail and was desperate to keep up. Keeping up became the sin that so easily entangles.

We weren't made to keep up. We were made to be free. To be who we already are.

When Jesus says "follow me," he calls us into his work, and we race to join him in the work of the kingdom, running as fast as our chain-laden legs will carry us. You see the problem, don't you? Whoever heard of someone running a race in chains? Yet this is exactly what many in the church are doing.

These chains become ankle weights. We grow accustomed to them, excuse them, work within their limitations. We begin to grow comfortable with them, perhaps decorate or even celebrate them. We eventually claim them as our *identity*, denying the possibility that these chains could fall away. How tragic, for despair is when we believe we will never truly change.

I'm here to tell you it's possible to believe that Jesus is the Christ, the Son of God; to believe he came and died and rose again; and yet still not experience freedom. It is possible to believe and still wallow in the pit. Who wants that?

When we become enslaved to anything, we miss out on a life of surrender and peace. A life where we experience the truth that God is enough. A life where God is the Good Shepherd who gives us everything we need. A life where we lack nothing.

Many of us in the church operate from a place of wounding. Some hide their wounds in shame. Others aim to prove themselves worthy. Many seek the approval of others; they take pride in the work of their hands. Consequently, we have created a culture of inadequacy and comparison in the body of Christ, causing many believers to feel a terrible pressure to strive. I wonder if Jesus looks at all our posturing, and says, "I didn't ask you to do that."

We cannot prioritize our doing before being, our assignment before healing, our service before freedom.

Have you noticed how much brighter a light shines in the dark than in the light? It took moving from Atlanta—the center of the buckle of the Bible belt—to New York City—the center of fame and fortune—to understand how *un*free I was. The first two years in Manhattan I slipped into the back row of the tiny church plant we attended on the Upper East Side. Our pastor taught in a tempered, shepherding tone with his rogue Australian accent, and I soaked up the promises of Jesus like a sponge. Promises of a life abundant, of being made new, of a hope reborn that won't disappoint. It was as if I'd never heard the good news before.

Every week I hid in the back row, sobbing during the sermon. I ran to the bathroom during the final prayer, before anyone saw my mascara-streaked cheeks. I had no idea why I was hurting so much. Looking back, I see it now—I was unraveling. I could perform no longer.

Those bathroom prayers at Trinity Grace Church were the beginning of the end of my striving. They were the prayers of a girl who longed for the rhythms of freedom, even if she didn't realize it yet. Jesus wanted to relieve me of this world's weight. He waited, just beyond the horizon, for me to be ready. He would come.

He would teach me to be free.

Becoming Free

At the end of each chapter, I'll offer a few questions and suggestions for you to consider. Grab a journal and a pen, and explore these prompts as honestly as possible. Allow these to link my story with yours. Allow them to be a gateway into an examination of your own life.

1. Do you remember a time in your life when you felt truly free? Perhaps you were in elementary school or newly married? Maybe you were a new parent. Whatever the case, write a few paragraphs describing this season in your life.

2. Sit in a quiet space and ask this question: When did bondage creep in? Ask God to show you, and sit in the silence as he provides the answer.

3. Prepare your heart for the areas of freedom we'll explore in this book. Consider praying this prayer: *Jesus, bring me into a place of true freedom with you. Show me the way back into your freedom.*

2

Free to Be Rescued

"If you are going to be used by God,
He will take you through a multitude of experiences
that are not meant for you at all,
they are meant to make you useful in His hands."
OSWALD CHAMBERS[1]

LONG BEFORE MARRIAGE, before children, before my freedom journey began, I marched off to college at Liberty University in Virginia, a fifteen-hour drive from my Florida home. I subconsciously chased liberté even then, although I only applied to the university because all applicants were promised a free sweatshirt. Others thought Liberty was too strict—back then the dress code required women to wear dresses and men to wear ties—but not me. I was used to rules, and the rules at Liberty were more lenient. The midnight curfew was a dream, an hour beyond my 11 p.m. curfew at home!

Gabe and I met my sophomore year and fell in love three years later. One night at an off-campus party, while trying to impress me with his dance maneuvers, Gabe sprained his ankle. When he fell, so did I.

I knew I'd found my dancing kindred.

Our love burned like a Roman candle: white hot and fast. Gabe's view of the world was as big as the sea, and I was caught up in all his dreaming. Our hearts were bigger than our brains, but that was okay. We were married three months (to the day) after he proposed, and zeal carried us through our first three years, until the fateful day our first son was born, our son with Down syndrome.

What once seemed so important to us no longer was, and something we'd never considered—what it means to be parents of a child with special needs—became front and center. Gabe left his successful career path as vice president of a leadership training company and came home to work from the couch. He was beginning his own freedom journey, and this was a step down that path.

Gabe's new career path was exciting. We started an organization, Q, which hosted events to equip Christians to engage our culture. As Q grew, thousands of thoughtful Christians gathered to learn in a new city each year. We convened in Atlanta, New York, Chicago, Washington DC, Los Angeles, Portland, Austin, Nashville, Boston, and Denver; we discussed what we were *for* as followers of Christ instead of what we were *against*.

Gabe was first to catch the itch to move to New York City. It was the center of American culture, the capital of new ideas. It was the perfect home for Q, he thought. I resisted for three years; how could a Southern girl leave Atlanta for New York City? Finally I relented, adopting the idealism that comes with any mid-life reset. We loaded three kids and two toy poodles into our minivan (a vehicle which is not hip anywhere, but is especially uncool when pulling into midtown Manhattan), but that's exactly what we did.

I thought New York would bring new adventure. I wanted to do something grand for God in the Big Apple. But instead of living out a life of grandiose meaning, I found myself melting down.

Moving to this city of eight and a half million people threw me into a tailspin. I was on an airplane over New York during my first panic attack; fear closed in, threatened to capsize everything. This first bout of anxiety set in motion a cycle that could not be reversed.

Anxiety became my fancy word for fear.

I feared God was not enough or that he didn't see my struggle. Had I known my anxiety was a gift, a kindness that would reveal and help heal the wounds hidden deep within me, I wouldn't have been so afraid of it.

The panic took over in trains, subways, elevators, and crowds. If you've visited Manhattan (or any large metropolis, for that matter) you know it's impossible to avoid these things. One day, panic set in as the subway doors closed. I tried to pry them apart, clawing at them with my hands. Coffee splashed on the ground; I shed my scarf and coat in a desperate attempt to breathe more freely. But the train took off anyway with me trapped inside it, engulfed in hot tears and desperate prayers.

When you go from being a high functioning individual to not being able to breathe on your own, you suddenly realize your smallness. Your *weakness*.

In the midst of this, I watched my husband, my unintentional foil. He practically skipped down the streets of New York, filled with clarity and purpose, an awareness I'd never known. I'd assumed the city would be a perfect place to recover my own passions, but that didn't seem to be working out. I wrestled with God in the snowy solitude of Central Park at dawn, where I walked each day that winter, searching for strength.

My anxiety attacks continued for almost a year. One Tuesday morning, friends gathered to pray that I would be delivered from fear and panic. Late that night, I woke as I'd done so many times before, unable to breathe, unable to speak. I could only grip my husband's arms while he interceded for me. Finally I found my voice and confessed my desperate need:

"God, rescue me; deliver me; I cannot do this without you."

In an instant my panic evaporated. My once shaking body grew calm. My breathing became normal, and my heart stopped racing. All was still. Nothing moved except my eyes, which were darting back and forth. In more charismatic circles, people would say God healed me instantly, but this Baptist girl had no language for it.

I'm not sure what I expected the night Light finally broke through the darkness. The truth is, I did not have a framework to understand the miracle of healing. I'd never given serious consideration to this type of rescue becoming part of my story. It conjured an image that made me feel unsure. I wondered how this kind of healing would impact me spiritually.

I'd watched many friends of my generation walk away from church after high school, not because the church wasn't full of well-intentioned hearts, but because they weren't experiencing the power of God—the power that transforms, heals, breaks chains, and literally sets us free.

I grew up thinking of the Holy Ghost as something akin to a boogey man or a creepy sheet-draped teenager with cut-out eyes on Halloween. I didn't study or understand the Spirit. It wasn't a significant part of my upbringing. The Spirit seemed mysterious, unpredictable. What if all this Holy Spirit stuff was just in our heads, I wondered.

Up until the moment God set me free from panic attacks, I did not believe I could be healed of depression and panic, even when friends laid hands on me and prayed for healing. Because mental illness ran in my family, I believed it was my lot in life. I was convinced I would have it all—panic attacks, claustrophobia, nervous energy, difficulty breathing. It never occurred to me to ask for healing, to stretch into the belief that such a thing was possible. Instead, I considered practical ways to manage my fear. I went through the motions of the Christian life, even though despair had replaced faith in my heart. And here's the thing about despair: It overtakes the place meant for hope. It steals the belief that healing is possible.

Despite my slavery to disbelief, God intervened in the early hours of a fateful September morning in 2011. In utter desperation, I asked God to heal me, and when I lifted my left hand to the heavens with a cry for rescue, healing came. I remembered how I tiptoed out of my apartment later that day, cautious and unsure. Did the healing take? Would the smothering begin again on my way to the subway? Days turned into weeks. I reported to my friends—*no panic yet.*

The city burst into living color as October trees lined the mall of Central Park with oranges, golds, and reds. I remember how my soul came alive again, how it slowly unfurled. I stayed in the present, absorbed each sunrise and sunset. *Is this what rebirth feels like?* I pondered. All the noticing and the beholding? How had I never felt this in thirty years of being a Christian? God and I seemed to share this secret in the middle of a bustling world.

I'd encountered healing, and I was swept up in it. I took my first step toward freedom in the admission of my weakness, and the acknowledgment of my inability to carry the weight of the world. God rescued me from panic disorder. The words of David took on new meaning, "In my distress I called to the LORD; I cried to my God for help. From his temple he heard my voice; my cry came before him, into his ears . . . He reached down from on high and took hold of me; he drew me out of deep waters . . . He brought me out into a spacious place; he rescued me because he delighted in me."[2] It was a rebirth of sorts, and I was a spiritual baby all over again, seeing the world in living color.

Even still, rescue felt strange. It was, perhaps, the first time I'd ever begged for anything from God, so even after healing came, I didn't use the "h" word. I feared hearing, "Sure, that's your story. Lucky you." Why was I healed when I didn't really expect it, when so many others have offered pleas for decades to no avail? It didn't seem fair. I knew God wasn't an alienating God, and he didn't rescue me because I had "enough" faith—in fact, it was quite the opposite. He'd found me in my deepest, darkest moment, in the desperation of my complete and utter surrender.

During the first eighteen months of my struggle, I couldn't see beyond my own problems. When healing came, scales fell from my eyes. I began to see the weight in so many others walking the city streets, just like me. I started watching people, studying their features, guessing their stories, and engaging on the rare occasion when someone would make eye contact.

When I was sick, I only looked inward. Through healing, I started seeing everyone else.

With a bit of trepidation, I began to share my story with close friends. This circle eventually widened to include new acquaintances, then advanced to anyone who'd take more than five minutes to chat with me. As I shared my story, women responded. As if unlocking windows into their souls, women seemed to feel permission to be honest with me about their struggles. We'd pray together, cry together. I caught a glimpse of God waking others to his desire and ability to meet them in their places of need. I saw healing start to happen in deep and powerful ways, more diverse than I'd ever imagined.

This wasn't my story of struggle; it was his story of rescue.

I wondered, could God use this to bring freedom to others? This was uncharted territory, but I was ready to follow the path he'd chosen. I trusted God would take my hand. He would lead and guide me.

Becoming Free

1. My journey into freedom began with a confession of my need for healing. Maybe you're facing poor health (mental or otherwise) in your own life. If so, in what areas do you need the healing touch of God? He invites you to confess your need to him.

2. Consider praying together with me that God would heal your needs. *Jesus, come to me in my need and bring healing and wholeness to every part of my life.*

3

Free to Be Called

The place God calls you to is the place where your
deep gladness and the world's deep hunger meet.

FREDERICK BUECHNER[1]

A YEAR BEFORE OUR MOVE to New York City, on the eve of my thirty-fifth birthday, Gabe surprised me.

"How about I send you to Denver, to spend a couple days with Pete?" he asked.

I knew what this meant. Almost a decade prior, our friend and mentor Pete had spent time with Gabe, unpacking his passions, burdens, and life story. They made charts and graphs, planned and prayed, and ultimately outlined the assignment God was impressing on Gabe. Together they gave language to his calling.

I couldn't have been more thankful for Pete's role in helping Gabe discover his true calling. But when Gabe suggested Pete meet with me, I immediately resisted. Our kids were four, six, and eight. I'd *almost* completed a decade of diapers and Cheerios and poop. The light at the end of the proverbial tunnel was growing brighter, and I wasn't sure I wanted anything other than a break.

"I don't want a calling," I retorted. "I want a piano."

Music was the foundation of my story. I learned Every Good Boy Does Fine, and All Cows Eat Grass—mnemonics for the musical staff—at age six. I wanted to reclaim this part of my story, even all these years later. I aimed to make music and melody again.

So Gabe bought me a used piano off Craigslist.

Looking back, I laugh. He was wise not to push. One person cannot force another to wrestle with whispers of purpose or compel her to pull back life's curtain and ask God to reveal that part of her story, especially when that other person is simply happy to survive Target by feeding her toddler crackers off the shelf. The idea of calling felt intimidating, overwhelming. Like God, Gabe was patient.

As I found my story of anxiety resonating with others, I became more open to a discussion on calling. Pete came to New York for a visit and walked me through the same process I'd previously resisted. In the first moments of our time together, Pete quoted Viktor Frankl, saying "Life is never made unbearable by circumstances, but by lack of meaning and purpose."[2] This made sense. I'd moved to New York subconsciously looking for meaning, after a season of "lostness." Meaning began to blossom, but not until *after* my season of panic disorder. Chasing meaning, I tripped over surrender, the place of releasing total control.

I learned surrender navigating a new city. I learned surrender in crippling panic attacks. I learned surrender in a healing prayer. I finally understood.

Meaning *follows* surrender.

Pete said, "Calling isn't limited to vocation, it's rooted in God's creativity and how he's designed us."

I considered the truth of his words. Our purpose began when God formed us, and he continues to call us as long as we have breath. The psalmist wrote it this way: "For you created my inmost being; you knit me together in my mother's womb. I praise you because I am fearfully and wonderfully made; your works are wonderful, I know that full well."[3] God appointed his purpose for each of us, even in our mothers' wombs.

I'd memorized all of Psalm 139 in college, drawn by the wonder that God's imagination was so vast, so creative, that no two of us are alike. God wasn't casual about establishing our talents; he ordained them before our days began.[4]

I considered the uniqueness of my own story, the path I'd taken from the womb, and as I did, I began to understand my calling. Before I was born, God knew I'd be a reader; he knew that in fourth grade I'd read sixty-two Nancy Drew books. He knew I'd be mesmerized by the power of a good story. He knew the reader in me would long to communicate, to tell stories. God knew I'd major in Mass Communications in college, that I'd love the art of sharing messages.

God knew more than my passions and talents, though. He also knew the ways mental illness would unfurl in my family. He knew I'd give birth to a child with special needs. He knew I'd suffer from panic disorder. But the story didn't end with my limitations and weaknesses. God also knew he'd equip me to use my gifts to share hope with others through my own brokenness.

As I unpacked my story and my unique gifts, I began to understand. *Calling is where our talents and burdens collide.* Our talents are our birthright gifts, the gifts that make our hearts sing, come alive. Our burdens are found in our stories, in what breaks our hearts. God was inviting me to use the gifts that made me come alive, to redeem the things that broke my heart.

As I shared this clarity with Gabe, it became obvious to both of us. I should start writing. What began as an article on the topic of mental health evolved into a memoir entitled *Freefall to Fly*. The story chronicled every detail of my crash and burn and invited readers to find meaning in their own surrender.

God wanted me to share his words with a hurting, needy world. God—the very God who formed me, who breathed life into me, who knew what I was capable of handling—would empower me for the work. He would equip me to use my gifts to share whatever words he gave me.

As children of God, we have a corporate calling to love God and make him known. What's amazing is that this calling looks different for each of us based on our talents and the burdens we feel for others. We don't have to stress about finding our "thing," but simply ask God to reveal his plans for us.

Calling begins with a caller! What a relief; calling isn't up to us.

Scripture is replete with examples of men and women stepping into their callings, and often, the one called by God is hesitant to trust or believe in this calling. Consider Jeremiah, the Old Testament prophet. God gifted him with ability and platform. While Jeremiah was serving the people, God tasked him with delivering a difficult message to the people of Judah: God was preparing an enemy to destroy Jerusalem because of the disobedience of God's chosen people.

It wasn't a pleasant calling, warning your people that the God who'd so often provided for them, who'd led them out of Egypt, was preparing for their destruction because of their sin. But Jeremiah was faithful and spoke up, recognizing his burden and the ways God had equipped him even before he was born. He understood that it was God who empowered his calling.

In the opening chapter of the book, Jeremiah describes it this way:

> The word of the LORD came to me, saying, "Before I formed you in the womb I knew you, before you were born I set you apart; I appointed you as a prophet to the nations."
>
> "Alas, Sovereign LORD," I said, "I do not know how to speak; I am too young."
>
> But the LORD said to me, "Do not say, 'I am too young.' You must go to everyone I send you to and say whatever I command you. Do not be afraid of them, for I am with you and will rescue you," declares the LORD. Then the LORD reached out his hand and touched my mouth and said to me, "I have put my words in your mouth."[5]

Jeremiah was hesitant to step into his calling. He waffled, hemmed and hawed, told God he'd picked the wrong man for the job. But God responded to Jeremiah's objections by assuring him he would equip the prophet. Taking God at his word, Jeremiah followed in obedience.

In the New Testament, Paul speaks directly to the fledgling church about its calling, encouraging the people to step into it. To the church at Ephesus, he wrote:

> As a prisoner for the Lord, then, I urge you to live a life worthy of the calling you have received . . . There is one body and one Spirit, just as you were called to one hope when you were called; one Lord, one faith, one baptism; one God and Father of all, who is over all and through all and in all. But to each one of us grace has been given as Christ apportioned it . . . So Christ himself gave the apostles, the prophets, the evangelists, the pastors and teachers, to equip his people for works of service, so that the body of Christ may be built up.[6]

In the same way, Paul wrote to the church in Thessalonica, "With this in mind, we constantly pray for you, that our God may make you worthy of his calling, and that by his power he may bring to fruition your every desire for goodness and your every deed prompted by faith."[7] Paul was very clear: through the grace of Jesus, we've been called to a specific purpose, and it is God who equips and empowers us for this purpose.

Callings are not one size fits all. Some of you may be called to teach, speak, and write. Others may be called to serve in the corporate world, or at home, or with your church youth group. Some of you may be called to missions of justice and mercy, to serving at the community pantry or the battered women's shelter. You may be a preacher, a teacher, or an extraordinary giver of resources. You may be called to serve in quiet ways, to exercise gifts of hospitality in ways that go unrecognized. You may be called to organize or administrate. You may be called to what some believe is thankless work, but in God's economy, it will be exactly where he wants you.

No matter your calling, God chose you for a mission, and he appointed a purpose for you well before you were born. This purpose is to bring glory to Jesus, to be his very hands and feet. And if the task is daunting, remember this: as he calls you, he leans in and whispers, "Don't worry; I'll empower your work."

Before my life began, God knew how the story of my life would unfold. He knew how the curse of Adam and Eve's fall into sin would affect me. He knew the burdens that would break my heart. Before my life began, he equipped me with talents. He identified my assignments. He called me to participate with him in the redemption of the world.[8]

For years, when the question of ministry surfaced, I'd shrug it off. Later, as people invited me to share my story, I looked at Jesus and told him he picked the wrong girl. It was one thing to share from behind my laptop screen, but it was quite another to share publicly. After years of being held down by my own limitations and weaknesses, it was a stretch to step into a new role. *Look at my mess,* I thought. *How could he ever use me?*

One day I confessed,

Jesus, I am afraid to press into my calling.

I feel ill-equipped on my best days and like an emotional train wreck on my worst.

I'm afraid I won't have what it takes to carry things out, or I'll shrink back and avoid what is difficult.

Help me know which assignments are from you and not just thoughts spinning in my head. Don't let me run ahead of your lead.

Please make it simple and plain.

In his graciousness, God gently responded: *Don't you see? I didn't choose the wrong girl. I've had grace planned for you all along.*

I realized God never picked the wrong girl for ministry. The enemy picked the wrong girl to mess with!

He worked to disrupt me, to whisper lies in my ear. He tried to convince me I wasn't good enough or compelling enough. But every attempt at harm, God turned to good. Every attack brought me before the throne. Every trial built my faith. Each time, Jesus came and whispered. Each time, he reminded me it was he who called me in the first place. I could rest there.

So I began.

I started saying yes to anyone who would ask. City after city, gathering after gathering, I spoke to women, opened Scripture with them, and we searched for God together. At each gathering, I noticed a shift in the room. Eyes brimmed with tears. Women were waking to a truth many of us forget: *We were destined for a purpose.* My newfound friends wanted to know, *Is it too late to know my calling?* Would they, in the words of Holmes' lament, "never sing but die with all their music in them?"[9] I felt their angst. I'd pined over those very same questions.

I replied to heartfelt emails and messages from those awaking to the whispers of God's voice, to glimpses of hope that meaning would come. These hopefuls were reframing passion in their minds and hearts, shifting toward faith and away from fear. A tide was turning. I jotted down the stories I was hearing, and I found myself listening for a God who calls me—who calls all of us—toward his specific plans and purposes.

One fall morning, as I sat on the living room rug of my Manhattan apartment listening intently for his voice, he showed me a picture. I saw women gripped with fear, prisoners living in unlocked jail cells. Even though the doors of their cells were wide open and they wanted desperately to come out, these prisoners were afraid to exit. Captivity was all they knew. But here and now, God would enable them to walk free. I readied myself for the role of cheerleader, prepared to rally them on to freedom. I began looking for my pompoms, but God interrupted my plans.

Free to Be Called

Hey, Rebekah. How about we start with you?

I didn't understand. Not at first. Wasn't I walking in new freedom? Wasn't I empowering others to name and identify their struggles, to walk into healing and transformation? I'd confessed my need for healing and received it. I knew my calling. I felt meaning and purpose. Wasn't I already free?

Soon enough, I'd realize confessing my need was only the first step. I wondered, *What more would he show me?* Jesus came low, whispered in my ear that he was working out something new. "There's a deeper spiritual healing coming," he said. *What did this mean*, I wondered. I would soon find out.

Becoming Free

1. Do you feel overwhelmed by the idea of calling? If so, let's start slowly. Take a moment to reflect on your talents, the gifts God established before you were born. List them.

2. Next, reflect on your burdens, the issues you feel drawn to address. What are the moments that changed your life, that broke your heart? List and describe them.

3. Ask yourself whether God has equipped you with these passions and gifts in order to respond to the burdens in your heart. Is there a way they connect? Could the intersection of the two reflect God's call on your life? Spend time in prayer, and journal what God might be speaking to you.

4. Is there anything that keeps you from pursuing your calling? List those things, and then confess them to God. Ask him to show you the slow and steady way to live into your God-called purpose.

5. Consider praying, *Jesus, please reveal your plans for my life, the calling and assignment you've prepared for me. Make me readily available to your prompting. Give me the courage to walk through the doors you open. Make your will simple and clear. Amen.*

4

Free to Confess

*I will no longer act on the outside in a way that
contradicts the truth I hold deeply on the inside.
I will no longer act as if I were less than the
whole person I know myself inwardly to be.*

ROSA PARKS[1]

$\mathcal{P}$LEASE, GOD, *heal my heart.*

The prayer surfaced without warning, and once I spoke the words, there was no turning back. A dam broke, releasing tears bottled up for decades. These five words surged repeatedly in rhythm as I knelt on the cold shower floor, tears mingling with the water streaming from above. Blame travel fatigue, or sleepless nights in random hotel rooms, or the weight of speaking on mental health issues. My heart was spent. I was at the end of my reserves. I wanted only Jesus.

I should have seen the signs leading to this moment. I'd wrapped up a week of teaching in California and stumbled back to my room for pj's and comfort food. As I was inhaling a post-speaking-event cheeseburger in a darkened hotel room, I began to watch a talk online by Ann Voskamp.[2] Ten minutes in, the Spirit spoke truth to my heart, and I sat bolt upright in bed.

Quoting Augustine, Ann spoke these words over the audience: "You have made us for yourself, O Lord, and our heart is restless until it rests in you." I'd had a restless, striving heart for as long as I could remember. But often, when my pursuits came crashing down, chronic unrest pushed me to doubt God's goodness.

Ann continued, "Those who keep score in life just want to know that they count. When you work for an audience of One, you always know that you count." Was I restless and anxious because I hadn't learned to serve this singular audience? Was I keeping score?

As I reflected on these questions, I awakened to the truth. I was still striving. After a speaking engagement, I'd often go back to my hotel room and second-guess my delivery, or worse, check the number of retweets on Twitter, likes on Facebook, or hearts in my Instagram feed. When the numbers spiked, I spiked. When they dipped, I dipped. I'd vacillate between feeling brilliant and doubtful, sometimes even invisible. *Had the audience liked me? How did I measure up? Was I enough?*

I finally understood. I'd awakened to my calling, but I still wasn't free. I'd learned the truth, discovered my gifts, and named my burdens, but I still wasn't whole. In some ways I'd cheapened my calling with a prettier version of striving. I'd relapsed into copying, competing, and comparing. Without freedom I was still wounded, and I would soon burn out.

I realized the humiliating truth: I was *desperate* for public affection. I was hustling for it. Although I was free from anxiety, I knew the truth—I was not operating out of freedom in every area of my life.

My heart was full of questions. I kept probing, half-asking God, half-asking myself, "Do I count? Do I matter?" Then I finally heard God's voice again:

You matter to me; is that enough?

Silence.

"For some reason I'm not doing this for an audience of one," I admitted.

So I'm not enough?

"Yeah; you are kind of not enough. Why is this the case?"

I heard the truth in my own spirit: I didn't believe God's love was enough. Instead, I looked to the size and response of my readers in order to feel loved. I'd been growing my platform—up, up, up—reaching for the next rung on the ladder. I relapsed into the performing ways of my past. I'd always wanted more. More affirmation. More success. More stuff. So I scrambled. I hustled. I earned. If I couldn't break the cycle, I would never be free.

The realization that I was still held captive laid me bare, and I collapsed to the floor, heaving huge sobs.

Please, God, heal my heart.

The words landed with weighted hope.

God was so gracious, so patient, so kind. My heart was broken. I'd spent years bandaging it, but the pain could only be healed by the One who created me, who fashioned and formed me. He gave me his eyes to see that I was still living in bondage, and that what held me captive was my deeper wounding. All my striving for success was an attempt to matter, to count.

Sitting on the floor, I confessed right then and there.

God, I'm sorry I've made the world's approval my idol. I'm sorry I care more about what others think of me than about what you think of me. I'm sorry that instead of believing my life matters simply because you say it does, I have put all my efforts into things that make me feel important. I confess I've been blind to my grief and hurt and the aching void only you can fill. You gently, in your perfect timing and love, have shown me this. What a gift! I praise you. Please forgive me and heal my broken heart. Make it new, as if it was never wounded.

Did I believe Jesus could do this for me? Do you believe he can do it for you? Do we believe he can make us new?

Many of us are not free because we have not confessed the sins that hold us captive, keeping us in bondage. *Confession is the gateway to healing, the route to freedom.* James teaches us this truth, writing, "Confess your sins to each other and pray for each other so that you may be healed."[3] What is confession? Confession means "[admitting] you have done something wrong, or [admitting] unwillingly that something is true."[4]

We could start with this simple prayer: *God, I'm sorry I don't live as if you are enough. I'm sorry I substitute achievement, or body image, or food, or sex, or anything for the freedom you bring.* If we felt the freedom to confess our sins, our enslaving habits, it would lead to the healing and freedom we so desperately want.

I believe God is looking at his church, and he's telling us, "You're it! It is you on whom my glory rests. There's no need to seek anyone else's approval." And we look up from our nonfat soy chai lattés while we scroll through Instagram, counting the number of hearts on a post, and we say, "Who, me?"

Yes. Yes, you.

You who raise your voice with your kids.

You who are addicted to social media.

You who "retail" your way out of depression.

You who question whether or not you have any real friends.

You who aren't certain your life really matters.

You with your insecurity, your brokenness, your anxiety, your desperation.

You.

You are the light of the world.

You are the salt of the earth.

You are the city on a hill that cannot be hidden.

Dare you believe it?

Christ says to us, *You are my holy people, whom I love. I came. I gave my life. I set you free. I've already done this. I've given you a purpose. I've made you to live in the freedom of that purpose.* Yet we are still hobbling through life, afraid to confess all the ways we push against this truth, because we can't even believe it. We continue to reach for the approval of our family, of our friends, of society.

If we want to be free, we have to move beyond confessing our need for healing. We also have to believe this truth: Christ came, walked this earth, paid the price, bought us, and set us free. He declares, *You are free; be who you already are.*

Most of us understand confession as a form of repentance, an admission of guilt and a request for forgiveness and healing. But confession has another meaning as well, one just as essential on our journey to freedom. Confession can also mean *declaring something emphatically,* such as our faith. Romans 10:9 says, "If you confess with your mouth the Lord Jesus . . . that God has raised him from the dead, you will be saved."[5] This verse is not just about confessing sin. It's about confessing that Jesus has come to save us in our bondage; he has come to set us free.

When we confess something with our mouths—such as our belief that God can forgive sins or heal us, or the fact we've been made free through the glorious gospel of Jesus—we plant truth deep in our hearts. It becomes a seed, eventually yielding a harvest. Faith is always the evidence of what we can't yet see; faith trusts what Jesus declares is true. Confession, then, is a specific form of faith.

Confession begins with repentance and ends with declaration.

We trust that even in the darkness of our own unbelief and sin, we'll look back years later and see how faith exploded from a mustard seed into a freedom song, a healing song.

This was certainly the case for me.

God was gentle with my confession. With kindness, he revealed the reason behind all my striving: In my youth, I believed my worth was determined by what I could offer. I felt rejected, unseen, unheard, unless I performed. So I put every effort into saying and doing all the right things to earn love from others and from God. Although I didn't have words for it then, I believed I was not worthy of love unless I earned it, especially God's love.

The pain of this revelation was a grace; it showed me all was not well in my soul. I realized no amount of public affection would heal my wounds. No number of roads traveled, cities frequented, books sold, positive reviews, or even souls healed would restore me. In those quiet moments, as I dialogued with God, he whispered this truth:

Public affection cannot heal private rejection.

I'd spent years trying to put a Band-Aid on my pain, but only the One who created me, who fashioned and formed me, could revive my broken heart. I grabbed my journal and began to scratch out this prayer of freedom:

Please, God, heal my heart, every broken part. Heal it FOR GOOD and set me free. I don't want to keep fighting the enemy's lies that I am still broken and wounded.

Can you make my heart new? Not just mended, but actually new? Can you make it whole, as if it were never broken?

This is the healing I am asking for. Not a patch job, not stitches, but a new heart that can only come through your healing and anointing power. A heart that prays bold prayers and believes bold things. One consumed with passion and purity and the pursuit of all that is holy.

Wake me to my bondage; help me cry out, "No more!" May the earth shake and the mountains tremble and the prison doors open so I can be set FREE.

Come in Spirit and power, heavenly Father. I will not be silent about this rescue. I will declare that your name is great, your mercies are ever new, and your grace and goodness extends to all generations.

In your most precious, compassionate name, Jesus, I ask all these things. Amen.

Jesus doesn't say you *can* be or *may* be or *will* be free. He says you *are* free.[6] Therefore, we must declare—we must confess—truths like the following:

We are adopted heirs of the throne, sons and daughters of a King.[7]

His love knows no bounds.[8] It is an everlasting,

all-consuming fire invading our hearts and minds when we allow it, and it turns our worlds upside down.[9]

No amount of loss or sadness or rejection separates us from his great and marvelous love.[10]

No amount of manipulating and toiling, of approval seeking, will ever increase his love for us, or bring us into right relationship with Jesus.

Freedom has already come.[11] It is found at the foot of the cross, where Christ took our lack upon himself and declared, "I am enough. I have bought you with a price and set you free."[12]

When I wrote my freedom prayer, I had yet to experience the full freedom that confession and healing would bring. But I believed even timid words planted in tears would reap a harvest.[13] My family will attest that I fall short of God's glory every single day, but my understanding of my freedom has completely changed:

The fall may be everywhere around us, but it is not in us.

Instead, it is Christ in us, the hope of glory.

Isn't this the point of the good news? When we confess our brokenness and receive the full pardon of Jesus, we are free.

Many in the church cannot fathom the kind of freedom Christ's pardon brings. We are so used to our prison cells, we don't even know we are still in them! The doors are wide open—Christ tore them off the hinges two thousand years ago. Many of us, though, still stand inside. My prayer is that we will begin to receive healing from our deepest wounds and discover that restoration brings true freedom. As we abide in God's presence, where he informs and sustains us, we can serve from a new place of freedom.

Confession, whether it be a confession of repentance or a declaration of truth, begets freedom. There is no shortcut or strategy.

This is how we run *free*.

Becoming Free

1. Do you believe the God who created the universe loves you and wants to know you? Journal your response to this question.

2. Do you find yourself striving for the attention of men, of women, of society at large? Do you find yourself seeking attention from everyone other than God? Journal your response to this question.

3. Ask God to reveal to you the areas in which you strive for the attention of others. Ask him to reveal the areas of sin that keep you from experiencing his love fully. Go slowly; allow the Spirit to bring those areas to mind over the span of several minutes. When he has done so, write out a prayer of confession and repentance.

4. What truths do you need to declare so you can live in freedom in these areas? Write them in your journal and review them often to remind yourself of what God has declared to be true.

5

Free to Thirst

The thirstier a man is, the more he'll prize a cup of water;
the more our sins break and burden us, the more
we'll treasure our Healer and Deliverer.

THOMAS WILCOX[1]

S THE HOLIDAY SEASON PROGRESSED, some friends gathered for our annual New Year's Eve tradition of good food and reflection. Feasting around the table on bacon-wrapped dates and chocolate with sea salt and almonds, we looked back on the previous year with mixed emotions. We toasted moments worth celebrating. We confessed moments of regret.

My favorite part of the evening—just before ringing in the New Year—is capturing the essence of the past 365 days in a single word. When it was my turn, without a second thought, the word fell from my lips—*light*. My friends looked across the table at me with enthusiasm. They'd remembered when my words were "rescue" and "retreat." Seeing I was in a new place encouraged us all.

I'd confessed my need for spiritual healing from the striving, the hustling, and the effort of measuring up. I knew the weight of darkness, how heavy it is, but this New Year dawned with *light*. I sensed God saying, "If I ask you to *be* light, I will make it *feel* light. Remember, Jesus tells us his yoke is easy to bear, and the burden he gives us is light.[2] I knew if I listened, confession by confession, Jesus would lead me into true freedom.

The bustle of a new year found us pounding the pavement in New York City. Truth came to me as I walked the streets to and from school drop-off each morning. I stopped to record phrases using the notes app on my iPhone every few blocks. God was feeding me truth, and my only job was to get it down:

Come to me when you are exhausted and weak, and I'll give you rest. Sit with me. Learn from me. I'll make your ministry easy again.

Don't confuse meekness with weakness; the poor in spirit inherit the kingdom of heaven.

We often insist our setting must change before we can live fully, but perhaps it won't change *until* we live fully.

Three weeks into the New Year, our college friend David, now a successful entrepreneur, came to visit. He fits the definition of *prophet* more than anyone I've known. A man who's as concerned about being grounded in the Word of God as he is about ensuring God's truth is known by everyone he encounters, David's boldness and clarity are inspiring.

After catching up on our lives and families over lunch, David followed Gabe and me around our apartment, Bible open, reading aloud Scripture after Scripture as a way of blessing our home. As we circled our 1,100-square-foot residence, he reminded us of what had stirred our hearts twenty years prior. He called it out like a big brother who could see a future that appeared foggy to us. We stayed up into the wee hours of the morning; praying, imagining, and dreaming of revival.

After David and Gabe walked out the door the next morning, I collapsed on our tiny kitchen floor, sobbing. I had no idea why I was crying, but these broken phrases came spilling out between breaths:

"I can't. I can't. I can't."

"Too big. Too dark."

"Ok. Yes. But God, please go before me and bring people around."

After an hour, I opened my Bible. I wasn't looking for anything in particular, but trusted the words of God would jump off the page for me. These words of Amos stung, needling their way deep into my heart: "'The days are coming,' declares the Sovereign LORD, 'when I will send a famine through the land—not a famine of food or a thirst for water, but a famine of hearing the words of the LORD.'"[3] The people of Israel were spiritually famished and dehydrated, the prophet wrote.

I walked to the window, looking from my small glass box in the sky over Manhattan's financial district, one of the wealthiest zip codes in the wealthiest nation in the world. I was struck with the weight of our spiritual dehydration. We were experiencing our own famine—we were a thirsty people, a people who'd forgotten the living waters only God provides. We'd forgotten his presence, traded it for achievement and personal profit. On the outside, society looked polished and happy, but its insides were crumbling. We were sick and emaciated, starved for the words of a powerful God. There could only be one cure. Taken aback and uncertain where this train of thought was going, I sensed God would reveal something if I could venture deeper and remain there.

Days later, I boarded a plane for a gathering in Florida. In the Sunshine State, thirty of us set aside time to gather and listen to God, to see what he might do in and through us. The timing could not have been more perfect.

The first night, after my roommate and I stayed up late swapping stories, I had a dream. Now, some dreams I completely ignore and chalk up to too much chocolate late at night, but this one seemed different. In my dream, I heard my friend (the one sleeping in the other room) calling me over. I stumbled from my bed toward her whimpering cries and found her tossing restlessly, talking in her sleep.

Then the wildest thing happened. In my dream I had the clearest sense of a random phrase that sounded almost biblical. It was crystal clear, as if God was speaking it directly to me: *Blessed are the broken who go to the water, and the rivers dry up for thirsty bread.*

I woke up from the dream, startled. *How weird is this?* I thought. Confused, I sat up. With no chance of going back to sleep, I followed my curiosity and Googled the phrase. I wondered, *What are the chances this actually means something?* Several results splayed across the screen, leading me to Joshua 1–12 and then eventually to Exodus.

Exodus tells of the Israelites' rescue from slavery. After they had been enslaved in Egypt for hundreds of years, God freed them by miraculous signs and wonders. But despite having been set free, the Israelites did not enter the Promised Land straightaway. Instead, they roamed the wilderness for forty years, grumbling against God and against Moses, their deliverer. The Exodus account records it this way:

> The whole Israelite community set out from the Desert of Sin, traveling from place to place as the LORD commanded. They camped at Rephidim, but there was no water for the people to drink. So they quarreled with Moses and said, "Give us water to drink."
>
> Moses replied, "Why do you quarrel with me? Why do you put the LORD to the test?"
>
> But the people were thirsty for water there, and they grumbled against Moses. They said, "Why did you bring us up out of Egypt to make us and our children and livestock die of thirst?"[4]

Although the Lord provided for the people in their physical thirst,[5] spiritual hunger and thirst were the norm during their desert wanderings. In forty years of wandering the desert, the stubborn generation delivered by Moses never understood freedom. They'd been slaves in Egypt their entire lives; captivity was all they knew. A *new* generation, their sons and daughters, would enter the Land of Promise.

God appointed only two people who were delivered from Egypt to lead this next generation into freedom. One was Joshua, the other Caleb. After Moses died, the Lord told Joshua it was time to lead his people across the Jordan River and into the Promised Land, a land flowing with milk and honey. This was the land where the

Israelites would no longer thirst, where famine and drought would no longer be the norm.

Following God's instructions, Joshua gathered the twelve priests who would carry the Ark of the Covenant—the dwelling place of God—and instructed them: "When you reach the banks of the Jordan River, take a few steps into the river and stop there."[6]

Arriving at the Jordan at sunrise the next morning, the men faced a raging river. (In the flood season, the Jordan River is twelve feet deep in some places, with currents reaching forty miles per hour.) The odds seemed impossible. But the Hebrews advanced, and as soon they stepped into the water, standing their ground on the riverbed in the midst of surging currents, God moved! As it was foretold in Scripture:

"And as soon as the priests who carry the ark of the LORD—the Lord of all the earth—set foot in the Jordan, its waters flowing downstream will be cut off and stand up in a heap."[7]

The raging waters around their feet began to recede. God held back the raging currents approximately nineteen miles upstream, until the waters stood up high into the sky. Picture a glass wall in the middle of the riverbed, not letting any rapids pass by. Can you imagine? As far as their eyes could see, the riverbed grew dry. God held the waters at bay as long as the priests stood their ground. The riverbed remained dry until the entire nation of Israel had crossed over.

Consider the priests responsible for leading God's people.

They stepped out in faith.

They waited.

God moved.

They stood their ground until everyone was safe.

I started to see connections to that crystal clear phrase I'd heard in my dream, *Blessed are the broken who go to the water, and the rivers dry up for thirsty bread.* Throughout Scripture, the broken were found going to the water. The people of Israel were led to the waters of God, ushering them into a new season of freedom. In the same way, God can hold back the waters and allow his people *today* to walk into freedom.

What does that look like for us? Are there places where God asks us to stand firm and hold our ground? What if our willingness to remain faithful while society screams for change brings a windfall of promise? Of blessing? Of freedom?

On that day there was partnership between God and man. God asked Joshua and the priests to step in, to stand firm, to hold their ground. God held back the waters as long as they remained steadfast.

And the thirsty bread?

Early in Jesus' ministry, crowds sat for hours in the hot sun to absorb his teaching. One day before Passover, five thousand assembled. Knowing their hunger, he asked for a boy's lunch—five barley loaves and two fish. He broke the bread, blessed it, and multiplied it. In God-like fashion, he gave the thousands enough to eat their fill with twelve full baskets left over.[8] This was a foreshadowing of God's lavish provision, offering exceedingly and abundantly above what we ask or think.[9]

What God begins with the natural, he fulfills with the supernatural.

Jesus fed the people on the mountainside that day with literal bread because he knew he'd need to reveal a different kind of bread the next day. This spiritual bread, the bread of God, would also be broken on a mountain, blessed and multiplied, for all who believe. Finally Jesus broke the news as if he could not hold back any longer:

"I am the bread of life. Whoever comes to me will never go hungry, and whoever believes in me will never be thirsty . . . For my Father's will is that *everyone* who looks to the Son and believes in him shall have eternal life."[10]

I can only imagine the earnestness in his eyes, his breath strained with the weight of these words. His physical body, our *bread*, would be beaten, stripped, whipped, speared, and broken so that we can partake and never be hungry again.

Furthermore, as Jesus was hanging on the cross, he said, "I am thirsty."[11] He thirsted because of our sin, our shame, our brokenness; he took it all so that we could be free.

Jesus is the thirsty bread.

Jesus first thirsted for us, for our freedom. I reflected on this biblical story and the significance of the phrase in the dark of my hotel room. We are hardwired to thirst. In fact, thirst is said to be the strongest of all human urges. When we are thirsty, we will do anything to be filled.

I wondered how much I thirst for God.

Did I ache for Him?

Long for his presence?

Desire his peace?

Burn for his compassion?

I understood that like the children of Israel, I'd spent years in the wilderness—years where I was spiritually dry and thirsty, looking to the wrong things to satisfy my longings, to be considered worthy. Even after my healing from panic and anxiety, hadn't I walked back into the slavery of striving, to my attempts at perfect Christian service?

Growing up in church, I did my best to obey all the right rules. When I failed, God seemed far off, and I felt undeserving of his love. Each time I vowed to try harder. I attempted holiness before grace, sanctification before justification. The rightness of my relationship with God was on *me* by my own choosing. The God I imagined shook his head in disappointment instead of straining his eyes across the hillside in my direction, arms spread wide, longing to satisfy the spiritual thirst of his daughter. In reality, he was willing to part the waters if I would only take a step off the bank.

I confessed to Jesus,

I'm one of the broken ones, you know.

For years I've loved seas and rivers, always drawn to the water.

But YOU are the living water, poured out readily as a healing balm whenever I come.

You are the thirsty bread, the bread of life that hung on a cross.

You uttered, "I am thirsty" even then, for my freedom.

Help me thirst for you in return.

Heal me in places I don't even know I need healing.

Show me what you see.

Show me what you want to set free.

I couldn't help but remember the woman at the well in John 4. Like me, she didn't know *how* to thirst for living water. She didn't even know she wanted it until Jesus pointed it out to her. He said, "When you drink the water I give you, you'll never be thirsty again." She immediately replied, "How do I get this water?"[12]

Jesus prompted her thirst then. He prompts our thirst now.

She continued, "Give me this water, so I don't have to keep coming back."

He responded, "Go get your husband."

Doesn't it feel like they are having two separate conversations? He's speaking about spiritual healing, and she's responding in the only way she knows how.

I wonder how often my chats with God sound this way. She wanted what she could see. He wanted what she couldn't see. We see our obvious needs: shelter, clothing, food, and water. But Jesus sees our spiritual needs: righteousness, forgiveness, salvation, and eternal life.

Jesus offered her living water, water that could quench a deeper thirst she wasn't even aware she had.

She believed, ran, and told everyone, "Come, see a man who told me everything I ever did. Could this be the Messiah?"[13] She knew he was; and she became the first evangelist.

Growing up, I never understood my longing for approval was really an unquenched thirst for Jesus and his unconditional love for me. But Jesus came and rescued me in my thirst. He freed me from anxiety, and now he wanted to free me from the spiritual weight of striving.

He led me to the banks of my own flooding Jordan River. There in my hotel room, I confessed I was still enslaved to my own works; I didn't know how to thirst for God alone. He asked me to put one toe in the water, promised he'd part those waters and lead me on to my own Promised Land of freedom. On the other side, he came to me just as he came to the woman at the well and offered me the waters of life. Those waters, I discovered, were a bubbling spring from *within me*. This spring of life quenched my thirst for love and acceptance.

He thirsted first, so we could thirst in return.

This understanding was another step in my journey to freedom. I'd tried to quench my thirst for the goodness of God by drinking the world's water, but I could never get enough. The world's water only created more drought and famine.

Instead, I needed to learn a holier thirst, the thirst for the presence of God, for revival, for small ministry in the church. I needed more of his goodness, not more of the world's acclaim, and I hoped to carry this goodness to a world thirsting for the same thing. God was already walking with me into the goodness; I just hadn't recognized it yet.

Two days after my epiphany, I headed back to New York, full of hope and expectation. I wanted to clear the way for Jesus. I wanted my thirst to drive me to perpetual confession, to continually draw me to him—the living water. I wanted Jesus to show me what his water would offer: forgiveness, rebirth, new life.

When we thirst for what Jesus offers, he shows us what he wants to set free.

I heard a simple whisper: "Get ready. I'll give you everything you need to push back the dark." I'd known I wanted him to revive his church, but I now realized revival began in individual hearts. I asked him to revive *me*.

Becoming Free

1. In the quiet, can you identify areas of your life where you thirst more for what the world offers than what God offers? Feel free to confess this to Jesus. He doesn't keep score or keep track. He simply wants to invite you into greater communion with him.

2. Have you desired to want more of God, to hear him, thirst for him? Ask God to grow this thirst, to give you the desire for him, to create space for this to happen.

3. Consider this prayer: *Lord, make me thirsty for more of you. As you grow my thirst, lead me to the water. Show me the ways you want to quench my thirst. You alone are the water of life.*

6

Free to Ask

*Some people think God does not like to be
troubled with our constant coming and asking.
The way to trouble God is not to come at all.*

D.L. MOODY[1]

MARCH ROLLED IN with a vengeance. Three feet of dirty snow was piled in the gutters of New York City with no sign of reprieve. It was the harshest winter I'd known, yet spring budded in my heart. Roots of new life grew deep, although the green leaves of freedom would not fully unfurl for a while. I claimed for myself the words of Psalm 1. I would be a tree planted by streams of water, and trust fruit would come when it was supposed to. I looked for clues of that coming fruit with expectation. Channeling my childhood hero, Nancy Drew, I became an amateur detective, looking and listening for evidence of what God was doing in and around me.

The church plant we were a part of, Trinity Grace TriBeCa, prepped for Easter, for celebrating the resurrection. We felt an urgency we couldn't explain to gather weekly in homes, get on our knees and pray. It was a tender time. I remember thinking, *I can only imagine the life forming beneath the harshest of winters. Spring might astonish us all.*

It was three years after my healing from anxiety, and my schedule required me to travel most Fridays, so I spent Thursdays praying and preparing. One Thursday while praying out loud, I paused mid-sentence and said something out of the ordinary.

"I sense that I'm supposed to ask for the spiritual gift of healing."

Whoa, I thought. *Did that just come out of my mouth?* My own words surprised me. I'd never felt prompted to specific action right in the middle of prayer. Of all things, a prayer for the gift of healing isn't high on the list unless you want to be criticized or ostracized. But it kind of made sense. I'd encountered many stories of suffering in my travels, and I was often left unsure how to best respond. Maybe this was a way God wanted to use me. I felt a pull to surrender.

I knelt down and simply obeyed without overthinking it, praying, "Jesus, you tell us to ask for more of the Spirit[2], so, here goes. I'm asking you for the gift of healing *if you want me to have it.*"

I sat in silence for a while. Yes, I believe God is the great physician; he showed himself to me as such. But I also couldn't explain it, and I was therefore uncomfortable talking about it. Even so, I sensed God was leading me to ask him for the gift of healing, so I followed his prompting.

Unsure of what to do next, I remembered the saying, "Angels whisper to a man when he goes for a walk."[3] I bundled up to battle the eleven-degree temperature, left my apartment building, and headed for the Hudson Riverwalk across the street.

The boardwalk was empty, thanks to a windchill in the single digits. With early morning go-getters already at work, I had the path all to myself. I walked south along the river toward the adjacent pier, alone with my thoughts. The winter morning was silent. I could only hear the waves lapping against the barnacles on the wood pilings beneath me. I gazed across the Hudson toward the Statue of Liberty, her verdigris silhouette interrupting the sky. I pondered the meaning of her arm held aloft, bearing a torch for liberty and freedom. She stood brave and strong, broken chains around her ankles, these words engraved inside the pedestal below:

> *"Give me your tired, your poor,*
> *Your huddled masses yearning to breathe free.*
> *The wretched refuse of your teeming shore.*
> *Send these, the homeless, tempest-tost to me,*
> *I lift my lamp beside the golden door!"*

It was clear, the need for freedom affects everyone.

Aren't we all huddled masses?

Jesus responds, *Come to me. I'll break your chains, whatever they are.*

Right then, gazing across the Hudson, I confessed:

I have no idea how this healing thing works.

Uncharted territory is scary.

Help me pray for healing any time you prompt me to.

Give me courage to pray with anyone who asks.

And above all, give me greater faith, your faith, to believe anything is possible.

Nothing is beyond the power of the cross and resurrection.

Some moments in life are God-directed. Not in a metaphorical sense, but in a literal, walk-along-the-boardwalk sense. These moments can feel random, even nonsensical. Sometimes it's almost as if God is asking us to follow him out of the apartment, out of the neighborhood, maybe even to the water's edge. I believed God was leading me somewhere—but where? Why did he direct me to ask for something so scary and big? Was he drawing me further into freedom?

Several months after I walked along the river, after I reflected on God's healing in my life, after I prayed for the gift of healing, I was answering questions publicly during an evening service. The moderator's penetrating questions made me feel uneasy. She wanted to talk more, and she pressed in.

Was I really healed?

Had I had any panic attacks since?

What did I think about healing?

Did I have a theological framework for it?

The Baptist girl in me squirmed and paused. I'd never fully experienced people laying hands on the sick, anointing with healing oil, or speaking words of healing. Any public discussion of the topic made me nervous and made my friends squirm. I told the audience, "I've never publicly talked about this because I don't want to alienate anyone. I know the discussion of healing is fraught with baggage. But if anyone here would like prayer for healing—spiritual, physical, mental, emotional—just ask. I'd be honored to pray with you."

I followed this with a shrug of my shoulders, a half smile, and this disclaimer: "I'm not promising anything, but it never hurts to ask."

Sheepish grins and muffled laughter filled the room. I trusted God's sovereignty and timing, regardless of how he would answer our prayers. I also harbored a newfound hope that God really does want us to ask him for things that seem impossible or beyond our understanding. I was convinced he wanted me to invite others into vulnerability—the vulnerability to *ask*.

The session ended, and I was sure everyone would exit as quickly as possible. Instead, women began to line up along the aisles and the back of the room. This was uncharted territory. It was as if we were all taking a risk together. We stayed in that room for two more hours, woman after woman in turn feeling the freedom to confess her need, to ask for healing.

We all have defining moments that change the course of our spiritual lives. Some decisions lead us astray, although we might not see the wake of the collateral damage for years to come. Others draw us closer to Jesus, bringing us into deeper intimacy and trust. Either way, we don't see the shift until we reflect much later on the moment that marked it. Looking back, I see how that night marked a change in the way God had called me to minister.

What if disciple-making is not just talking *about God*, but inviting others to talk *to God*, to confess, repent, and then, with boldness, to petition him? What if disciple-making is about giving people the freedom to ask, no matter how big or impossible the request?

Scripture tells us the intense prayer of the righteous is a powerful weapon against sickness.[4] But healing isn't one size fits all; it's not a silver bullet or a magic pill. It is mysterious and elusive, captivating and enthralling, believable and unbelievable.

One thing is for sure: the way people in Scripture experienced healing looks different than what most of us experience today. Since we can't explain how healing actually works, we ask God to heal us "if it is his will," and then surrender to the outcome. Is that what he intends?

Yes, partly. But Scripture also instructs those who are suffering to pray, for those who are sick to confess their sin *and* sickness, to call the elders for prayer and anointing. Here's the key:

*We aren't responsible for the healing (or whatever seemingly impossible thing we are asking for); we're only responsible for the **asking**.*

Then comes the tricky part. After we ask comes the silence, the waiting. We've mustered up the courage, confessed our need, uttered the words, and left it all hanging like a stale refrain in the air. Then come the questions:

Will we wait for God?

Will we trust him?

If there is any comfort, know this—Jesus was in a similar place in the garden of Gethsemane. Knowing he was about to be put to death on the cross, he prayed, "Father, if you are willing, take this cup from me; yet not my will, but yours be done."[5] He asked God for a path around the pain, but then came the silence. In the silence, he followed the will of his Father into suffering. Jesus was crucified before he was resurrected. He knew the glorious plan of the Father could be trusted, even if it meant his death was required. In his faithfulness to walk through the pain, he conquered sin and death.

Maybe you've asked God for something, but only heard silence for many years, and it feels like your mustard seed of faith isn't growing.[6] Maybe you've felt faithless and condemned. Or perhaps you've felt as if God isn't interested in what is happening with you. Maybe your heart feels abandoned, rejected.

I don't know why God answers some prayers immediately and not others. It's a mystery. What I do know with full assurance is this: God has given us the freedom to ask him for anything—anything. Perhaps in God's economy what's most important is that we have the freedom and faith to ask.

What if we lay aside our concern about the results of our prayers?

What if we simply confess and declare what we have been given—the freedom to ask?

What if we begin to confess our needs to God, to ask again, with our whole hearts, for whatever we need?

How many of us are slow to ask, whether out of doubt or fear or even pride?

Asking requires much.

For starters, asking often requires an admission and confession of need, an acknowledgment that all is not well. Asking also requires us to *do* something, to participate in whatever God wants to do. Finally, asking requires us to entrust what is beyond our control to the One who controls all.

Asking awakens our holy imagination to God's divine intervention.

Asking says, "I cannot fathom how you would do this, but I trust you are able. So I lay aside what I can understand, and I embrace your promise and mystery of healing."

Being free to ask God for anything means trusting him the way a child trusts—openly and unreservedly and expectantly. It means not holding back. And isn't that the crux of our faith?

Months after holding that first impromptu healing after-party, I gathered with one hundred women at a retreat in Orange County, California. An adorable girl in her early twenties approached, telling me a group of women had been praying for forty days leading up to this retreat. Since God does not abandon an expectant heart, I knew he would show up.

The event was business as usual. I spoke of anxiety and depression, abiding and release. We went to bed, and the next morning I landed on healing. I camped there for a while. One woman said she'd asked for healing for ten years but had not experienced it. She wondered why. It was an open discussion, so another woman responded, pointing out that even Paul had an unresolved ailment.[7] Another woman jumped in, saying, "God doesn't always want to heal us." You could hear a pin drop. The Lord held my tongue; what could I offer?

After staring down at my wedges for some time, I cautiously began to speak, knowing I was stepping into the controversial waters that surround conversations about spiritual healing.

"We have these two things," I said. "What we experience, *and* what we read in the pages of Scripture. From what I can tell, Jesus never denied anyone who asked for healing during his ministry."

I explained that in John 5:6, Jesus asked a man, simply and plainly, "Do you want to be healed?" It wasn't a trite question. I can imagine his tone, his meaning. I believe he was asking, *No, really, do you?*

Or do you want to lie there, trying to manage your pain? Do you really want to be well? Because if you do, it will cost the rest of your life. You'll no longer be a victim. You'll no longer be able to agree with the lie that you are broken and crippled. Instead, you'll say, "I once was blind, and now I see! Maybe he's the Son of God."

Feeling the need to press into their very specific and valid questions, I went on,

"And as for Paul and his thorn in the flesh—didn't even he *ask* for healing? Didn't he *ask* for wholeness?" Regardless of the results, he still asked.

I explained how in his second letter to the Corinthians, Paul tells us God allowed this thorn in the flesh to teach him humility, to protect him from deceit. Paul asked God to remove his thorn, and God offered him a humble heart instead. Sometimes we ask for a healing we can see, and God offers instead a heart-healing we can't see. So, yes, it seems sometimes God has a purpose for allowing our brokenness to continue. Still, we confess our need for healing and wholeness. We pray against the brokenness of the world.

I concluded, "The truth is this: Scripture says we can ask God whatever we will, and yet we don't often live into this freedom, particularly when it comes to healing. We don't believe Jesus can really heal, do we?"

When I finished, I stood silent, waiting for a response.

Tears flowed. You could cut the tension in the air with the knife.

One woman cautiously raised her hand and asked, "Do you think we don't ask because we don't have enough faith?"

Her question forced me to reflect on my own story. Sure, I'd hosted small group Bible studies, memorized Scripture, planned marriage retreats, led worship, even worked on a church staff. Yes, I prayed God would heal me of my panic attacks, but I didn't expect him to do it. Not really. I was afraid he would not answer my prayer.

Was I afraid of disappointment? Yes. I feared my heart couldn't handle it. So I gave Jesus plenty of disclaimers just in case he didn't feel like healing me. My prayers for healing were timid, tentative, because I lacked belief.

Convicted, I cautiously and soberly responded, "If the same Spirit who gives power and authority to heal is the Spirit that brings conviction of sin, perhaps we should pause our prayers for healing and instead utter prayers for repentance. Yes?"

Women flooded the front of the room and fell to their knees, asking God for forgiveness. One confessed bitterness and asked for healing from the grief that followed her husband's suicide. Some, broken-hearted for their sick teenagers, prayed for spiritual repentance for their sons and daughters. Hearts were bared, and as confessions were spoken, prayers for healing followed.

Confession opens the gates for healing to rush in.

First, the healing was spiritual. But then, women began to ask for the healing of mental, emotional, and physical ailments. As I knelt among them, I heard their cries and prayers of deliverance. Anxiety and depression were lifted. Heaven never felt closer than that moment.

Heaven bends low when we have the freedom to ask.

The asking—sometimes it's the hardest part. Do you feel this? We second-guess God's love, his faithfulness, his power to heal, restore, and provide. But Scripture teaches us to ask. In Matthew, we're taught,

"If two of you on earth agree about anything they ask for, it will be done for them by my Father in heaven."[8]

Mark records it this way:

"Whatever you ask for in prayer, believe that you have received it, and it will be yours."[9]

Luke points to Jesus' teaching, saying,

"For everyone who asks receives; the one who seeks finds; and to the one who knocks, the door will be opened."[10]

The gospel of John records these words of Jesus,

"I will do whatever you ask in my name, so that the Father may be glorified in the Son."[11]

Maybe you've never experienced the freedom to ask for healing and wholeness, for deliverance from sickness, depression, or addiction. Maybe you've second-guessed the power of God and thought, *This is just the way it is.* But God our Father responds with love, power, and healing.

Today, invite God to visit you in your need. Invite him as the women in Orange County did that Saturday morning. If you do, you may find new freedom. How do I know? Because I've experienced first-hand the power found when we embrace the freedom to ask.

Becoming Free

1. Do you pray with closed hands, holding on to the fear of disappointment? If so, why? Journal your response.

2. What would you ask God, if you felt free to ask for anything? Even something so big it seems impossible?

3. Consider going for a walk. While you walk, ask God to show you any faith barriers, anything that keeps you from asking him to provide for all your needs, whether spiritual or physical. Write a prayer of confession, listing those barriers and asking him for what you need.

7

Free to Begin Again

Be like the fox,
who makes more tracks than necessary,
some in the wrong direction.
Practice resurrection.

WENDELL BERRY[1]

WHEN WE LEFT ATLANTA, I left everything I'd ever known—the genteel South, the sweet summer air, the landscape dotted with churches on every corner. New York represented transience and unsettledness, as seventy-five percent of the city's population are renters. People came and went each year. Just as relationships grew deep, friends moved away for career changes or family considerations. Then a new batch of friends entered.

Gabe and I were ready for radical change, so we sold the majority of our possessions when we moved to Manhattan. In the beginning it felt freeing—the maintenance of our things felt suffocating—but ridding myself of the comfort of the familiar also left me without a safety net, forcing me to see the truth: my soul was bankrupt. In the South, I'd leaned so heavily on stable friendships and an established home that when they were yanked away, I was lost without them. Overwhelmed by this reality, I begged God to return things to the way they'd been. Seller's remorse.

It was not possible for us to return to Atlanta, of course. We'd already jumped. Some things cannot be undone, especially if they were supposed to happen all along. So I gave in, submitted to the rhythm. Over the following weeks and months, I began to settle into the city. I had no house to hide in, no security blanket of old friends. It was just our little band of five and our apartment. I was lonely in those early days, but my soul began to be filled once again as I ran along the Hudson River at sunset, as I read poetry by lamplight, and as our little family grew closer in this big, new, wonderful place.

For some reason Gabe and I sensed New York City wasn't to be our permanent home. The first time our lease renewal was slipped under the door, we asked each other, "Are we up for another twelve months?" Our cautious response was, "Yes. I believe we are."

This conversation played on repeat year after year. For the first couple of years, we agonized over the answer. Each instance offered a fresh chance to opt in or out, but we always felt convicted to stay, not to run or retreat, no matter the struggle. Every year, we threw ourselves back into the work of loving the city with our whole selves.

Even so, we struggled with loneliness, with the difficulty of maintaining a family in Manhattan. We knew running from our struggles never solved any problems. God held us close, teaching us to rely on his peace while he extracted from our lives the things that threatened our freedom to rest in him alone.

Sometimes it takes being stripped of what is familiar, giving everything up, to be reminded of who we truly are. As my faith grew vibrant and free under his watchful keeping, God used New York City to show me I'm brave and independent. Falling isn't so scary once you lean into the wind. After all, that's how baby birds learn to fly; they freefall to fly.

One night I emerged from the subway into the crisp winter air. The Big Apple swelled with holiday lights and the hum of countless shoppers. I ducked east onto a quiet side street at Sixty-First and Lexington, and a thought hit me: *I am so small.*

I looked up at the night sky. There were so many lights I could barely see the stars, but I knew they were there, brilliant and endless. And here I was, a mere speck in the vastness of the universe.

But along with the revelation of my smallness came the conviction that the God of the universe saw me, held me. In that moment my smallness felt precious, important. Held by the city, by a God who was just beyond sight, I sensed that *home is wherever God is.* And God is ever with me.

With this epiphany, it became easier for me to relax my clenched fingers and begin to really *live* in our new home. Over time the city of New York, her streets, her people became my love. As I served on church planting teams, first on the Upper East Side and then downtown in TriBeCa, my faith grew. Just two blocks from where the twin towers fell, our core team walked the streets and asked for God's renown to come in fresh waves. We asked him to surround our city with Light, to bring life from the ashes of the terrorist attacks of 9/11.

New York is known for its abandoned historic church buildings, so folks were perplexed when our team started a new church. Our church had no building, no place to call home. We met all over the city—in public parks, public schools, waterfront piers, rooftop gardens, and even in Taylor Swift's apartment building. We were living proof that the church—like its Christ, the homeless man—does not call the brick and mortar *home*. The church finds its home where the fire of the Spirit abides in the hearts of God's people. This was a kind of faith I could embrace forever.

Gabe and I were thriving, scootering around the city between meetings, coffee dates, and late dinners. But the same could not be said of our three kids. Cade's elementary school years were a dream, and his teacher might have been a literal angel. She advocated for a mentoring program. Kids applied in droves to tutor her special needs students. They read books together, cooked together, danced together, partied together. Cade was a ladies' man, as evidenced by his fifth grade graduation picture with pretties surrounding him on all sides. He was loved and accepted.

Middle school was quite different. Everything changed his sixth grade year. The school didn't have other children with Down syndrome, and Cade didn't interact with any children except for those in his special needs classroom.

We'd been in New York for four years when Cade suddenly wouldn't get out of bed in the mornings. A social bug, he'd always leapt out of bed, excited for the school day. I grew concerned when his reluctance to go to school continued day after day after day. Then one morning I received a call from Cade's school. Cade had a stomach virus, and I needed to pick him up from the nurse's office. When he arrived home, Cade magically turned into all smiles. Strange.

The next day, it happened again. Once again Cade did the happy dance when he entered the apartment. Day after day this continued, so I took him to his doctor for tests. The results showed nothing suspicious. Apparently Cade could vomit on demand, and he was using this talent to avoid the stresses of middle school life.

As if this wasn't enough to convince Gabe and me that God might be leading us to move again, Kennedy and Pierce were facing their own challenges. Three elementary schools between Atlanta and New York was more transition than their precious first-day-at-a-new-school spirits could sustain. Pierce was outgoing and friendly, but kids teased him if he mentioned God. When Kennedy was called "sexy" on her first day of second grade, she didn't want to return the next day. Of course she did, but I paused and pondered whether or not the New York life was sustainable for all five of us.

During this season I had the most vivid dream. Gabe and I were driving on a highway, back into the city after a weekend away. Our kids were traveling with us, but they were riding in a separate sidecar. As we approached the exit before ours, I watched as the sidecar detached and entered the off-ramp heading to Brooklyn. Gabe and I maintained our course toward downtown Manhattan. We smiled and waved at the kids as if everything was fine. But as I watched the sidecar fade in the distance, as I watched my children round the corner and disappear from my sight, I panicked. "Gabe, where are they going? How could we just let them ride off? We have no way to reach them. No way to contact them. They'll be lost!"

I awoke terrified. My dream felt like a warning, an omen. How did Gabe and I get here, living as if everything were fine and normal, completely oblivious to the toll the city was taking on our children? I told Gabe about my dream, and as we talked, we agreed a ministry requiring us to abandon our children was not a ministry of freedom. I told Gabe, "Cade seems so alone right now." His isolation was keeping him in bondage to anxiety, to stress, to puking on demand. Our ministry in the city was beginning to extract a high cost—our children were suffering. Perhaps God was preparing us for something distinct in our future.

Gabe and I had upbringings far different from our children's. We were both raised in the church. We were surrounded by Christian teachers and Christian friends in Christian schools who also lived in Christian neighborhoods. We attended potlucks and missionary banquets and Awana speed races where we whittled our own racecars from blocks of wood. We sewed patches on blue vests, signifying our Scripture memory accomplishments, and competed in sword drills. I wore culottes to weeklong revival meetings and watched *A Thief in the Night*, a movie about the rapture.

It was the silo of silos, this upbringing. Please understand, I don't regret an ounce of my upbringing. Sure, the way I live out my faith has changed, my outreach methods have changed, but the Word of God has not. The Word was hidden in my heart long ago and grew my mustard seed faith. I'll forever be indebted to my parents for teaching me about Jesus, and I'm grateful to have been brought up in a church that served people well.

Gabe and I viewed New York as The Great Reset of our lives. We wanted to know: *Would our faith connect with those who grew up in this hip, urban culture? Would it even make sense? Could the gospel possibly be good news for someone who'd disregarded it long ago, or who'd never heard it in the first place?*

While these were all great questions to grapple with, the call to parenthood now arrested our hearts, becoming our primary focus. Were we stewarding the time for which God had entrusted Cade, Pierce, and Kennedy to us? Were we training them up in the way they should go?[2]

Scripture teaches children are "like arrows in the hands of a warrior" (a Psalm that inspired Gabe to name our middle child Pierce) and "blessed [are the parents] whose quiver is full of them."[3] We wanted to raise children who would pierce the hearts of people for Jesus. We only had nine years left before our children took flight, nine years to teach them how to freefall into their own new beginnings. It was a blink away, so we confessed to God and each other that we needed to make a change.

As we considered where we might plant our family for the years to come, Nashville, Tennessee, kept moving to the top of the list. The South had always felt like home. I grew up in Florida, met Gabe at college in Virginia, and we'd spent our first thirteen years of married life in Atlanta. Southern roots run deep.

It's funny how God works. Fifteen months prior to my dream, our team decided to host the annual Q Conference in Nashville. We made multiple trips to Tennessee throughout the year and began to ask, "Could this be where we land?" My immediate reaction was *no*. Don't get me wrong. The horse farms outside of Nashville are dreamy, and the rolling hills are picturesque, but I couldn't accept the thought of starting over again. I was afraid the comfort of the South would cause me to feel complacent. Would I move backwards spiritually—would I return to legalism and guilt and striving? The discomfort and struggle I experienced when we moved to New York had forced me to a new place of dependence on God. It gave me an understanding of God's presence and power, his healing and revelation, and his longing for us to live and thrive in relationship. I learned that when we cry out, he draws near. I was terrified of losing this dependence, for there I'd found rescue.

As we considered this decision for the next few weeks, I awoke each morning full of fear and doubt. The truth is, the challenges of New York had caused me to adopt the belief that my faith grew best when life was difficult. Subconsciously, martyrdom had become the foundation of my spiritual growth. It seemed God drew close when things grew difficult. In those times I was most aware of my deep need for him. I had yet to experience a vibrant daily relationship with him that wasn't tethered to struggle, and the struggle of New York City was palpable. New York was my city of surrender and healing. I'd found my voice through teaching and writing. What would happen to my faith in the comfort of Christianville?

I committed the matter to prayer, and confessed, *The tension of indecision takes such a toll. The unrest in our family wreaks havoc in my heart. It cripples me, robs my joy. I'm afraid to begin again, to risk again in a new city. Is this the right decision? Help me see what you see.*

I listened for God's whispers. He gently reminded me that my freefall into his grace was not because of New York, but because of *him*. Manhattan was only the setting that caused me to reconsider everything I thought was important in my life. Once I released the things I valued, whether influence, possessions, reputation, I found Jesus in the surrender. God assured me that what he began there—my confession, his bending low—was a union, and he could continue it anywhere. In fact, he'd restore the years of loss with new life and joy. I tucked that promise into my heart and held it tight.

I knew obedience had required me to *come* to New York City, but I'd never thought it would require me to *leave*. Would this next chapter in our lives be one of harvest? Abundance? Joy? It was almost too much to comprehend. But once Gabe and I made our decision, peace entered, and I shifted my focus from what we were leaving to where we were heading.

We shared the news with our closest friends in New York City and elsewhere. Getting our decision out there felt like complete release. Three days later we gathered with new and old friends at a large retreat hosted by our friend Bob. The weekend ended with a celebration dinner. Bob, who always had something up his sleeve, invited us to take a seat anywhere we liked, and announced there was an anonymous handwritten note under each person's plate. I reached under mine and read these words:

My beautiful, beautiful, beautiful child. You are the one. The one I have always been passionate about. Make your home in my arms. Rest. Stay. Feel my love pour over you.—Jesus

Psalm 139 says,

> "You have searched me, LORD, and you know me. You know
> when I sit and when I rise; you perceive my thoughts from
> afar. You discern my going out and my lying down; you are
> familiar with all my ways . . . Where can I go from your Spirit?
> Where can I flee from your presence? If I go up to the heavens,
> you are there; if I make my bed in the depths, you are there.
> If I rise on the wings of the dawn, if I settle on the far side of
> the sea [even New York City], even there your hand will guide
> me, your right hand will hold me fast."[4]

Wow. Can you imagine? God searches for us. He seeks us out and
finds us. In fact, the Trinity embodied this very concept in the
person of Jesus. He came on a search and rescue mission; he came
to make his home *with* us, to be with us. What does he say of home
for those who live into his mission, who confess and believe in him?
Jesus told his disciples, "Anyone who loves me will obey my teaching.
My Father will love them, and we will come to them and make our
home with them."[5]

As we follow Christ and confess the truth that he is our home, he
makes his home *in* us. He leads us into our true home, a place of
union with him. What a promise.

I could run from city to city, apartment to apartment, opportunity
to opportunity looking for *home*. A house or apartment is a sign

of provision, but the only home that will *keep* me is Jesus, safe in his arms. He is always there, even if just beyond my sight like the stars over the skyline. He is in my coming and going, in my lying down and my going out. He'll make home with me, whether I am in Nashville, Manhattan, or Timbuktu. Wherever I make my bed, he'll be there.

This is the beauty of our God. *He is our home.*

Confessing that my true home is found in Jesus ushered me into the freedom to begin again. The God who rescued me in Manhattan would always be with me. No matter where I moved, I would never be far from home.

Over the new few months, confirmations surfaced that God was indeed leading us to move, strengthening our sense that we were to live out the next phase of our lives in Nashville. Looking back, I cannot imagine our story without New York in it. Those years were the most formative of my adult life. There, God taught me a most valuable lesson—our true home is wherever God leads, and true freedom is only found there.

Becoming Free

1. How would you describe home? Is it more than a place to you? What does it represent?

2. A new beginning may not mean leaving your home or your employment, although those things may be tangible expressions of starting over. Ask God to show you the ways in which you need to reorient to him, the ways in which you need to begin again.

3. Are there moments you've made "home" more about possessions than people? More about places than the person of Jesus? I know I have. Feel free to confess this, if you've struggled in this area. There's no condemnation here; Jesus wants to free you to see a house as provision but people as the prize.

4. Consider praying this prayer: *Jesus, teach me how to begin anew, how to care more about finding home in you. Help me see that you are my true home, and that you are always with me, no matter where I go.*

8

Free to
Wait

Patience is not an absence of action;
rather it is timing.
It waits on the right time to act,
for the right principles, and in the right way.
FULTON SHEEN[1]

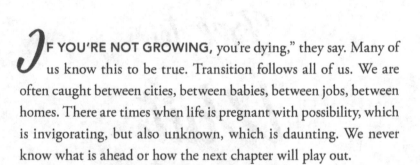

"IF YOU'RE NOT GROWING, you're dying," they say. Many of us know this to be true. Transition follows all of us. We are often caught between cities, between babies, between jobs, between homes. There are times when life is pregnant with possibility, which is invigorating, but also unknown, which is daunting. We never know what is ahead or how the next chapter will play out.

July swept in with humid heat, the kind that suggests pools and popsicles, so Gabe and I gratefully dropped off our three kids at summer camps. After making bunks and unpacking duffles, exchanging tears and hugs, the two of us drove off, waving wildly from our van. Within minutes, we looked at each other with giddy grins. We'd used all our mileage points and booked flights to Ireland for a week of vacation all by ourselves.

Sounds great, right? But there was a glitch in our plan. Moving Day was just two weeks away, and we still didn't have a place to live in Nashville. For the past three months we'd exhausted ourselves searching for an apartment. Because we needed to enroll Cade in a school that could accommodate his needs, our search for a rental was confined to a narrow zone of streets. It didn't help that we needed to rent an apartment that would allow us to bring our two toy poodles. Bless their poor matted heads, every application was denied. I grew more stressed and anxious by the day, but our flights were booked, so off we went.

Our vacation began peacefully, full of sightseeing and adventure. We rode bikes at dusk through spooky forests, toured the Titanic memorial in Belfast, cut crystal in Waterford, and played par three golf in front of a legendary pub. Over legs of lamb, we listened to local Irishmen turn stories into tall tales we weren't sure we could believe.

Then, a couple of days into the trip, Gabe and I began to bicker. He rose to the challenge of right-seat driving on the left side of the road. He hugged turns as if qualifying for NASCAR, accelerating through green hills, past crumbling castles and wayward sheep. We argued about directions on our three-hour drive to Belfast, what time bikes were available to rent, and whether to visit Powerscourt Gardens or the Cliffs of Moher. Stress was the culprit, and we both took the bait.

By bedtime on the third night, the argument snowballed. Gabe fell asleep mid-sentence, and I lay back on my pillow, staring at the ceiling. Why were we arguing? This was our one annual chance for recalibration *sans* kids, and we were ruining it. Desperate for answers, I considered staying up late to journal. (Writing usually grants me insight I don't find any other way.) However, fatigue won. I couldn't move another muscle and offered a request to the heavens. *God, please show up in my sleep.* I closed my eyes and immediately heard: "The LORD is my shepherd; I shall not want."[2]

I shall not want. For anything? Not for food, shelter, or clothing? Not for security, safety, or provision? What about a place to rent?

In Matthew 6:33, Jesus says to seek first his kingdom, and all the rest will be added. For the last eight months, I'd been on my knees, asking God to speak loudly. Wasn't I seeking his kingdom? Why were we so close to Moving Day and still in need of a place to live? Why hadn't God met our need for an apartment? Gabe and I were apartment renting ninjas by now. We'd spent six solid months on Streeteasy.com, a rental website, before moving to New York. We'd found an apartment in the largest city in the United States—surely finding an apartment in Nashville shouldn't be this difficult? Why were we living in limbo? This was an obstacle I didn't understand.

When we decided to move, I convinced myself that the wait for permanence and putting down roots was over. Now I realized it would continue. Could I wait on Jesus to meet our every need? Could I make Jesus my only source of security, comfort, and provision when everything else seemed to be falling through? The testing had begun.

The truth is, I wasn't merely waiting for the ideal housing situation. I was waiting for an answer to a larger question: *What was the point of all the moving?* Leaving Atlanta for New York City, then leaving New York City for Nashville, I felt caught in a loop.

What was God doing? I wanted to know the master plan. Just when we were beginning to see glimpses of fruit from our labors in New York, our kids led us out. We were beginning again, but I realized the questions would continue. We were no more certain of the future than when we'd arrived in Manhattan four hazy summers prior.

I brought my confusion before God in prayer a few days before the move and heard him say, "Get your house in order; you're going to battle." But hadn't we *been* in battle? What about the last four years of fighting to survive? What about the days I'd spent rocking in a fetal position in my closet, wondering, *Will I always struggle with depression?* What of those tears? Were they just boot camp?

Confused, I pleaded, "A battle for what? What's at stake?"

He gently responded, "My church."

I didn't have language for *awakening* then, but I sensed what God meant. I'd hoped for greater revival, yearned for a greater outpouring of the Holy Spirit, and from the cries of desperation in the hearts of God's people, we were beginning to see whispers of it in New York. In my arrogance and ignorance, I couldn't imagine that this same kind of desperation, this hunger and thirst, existed in the buckle of the Bible belt. After all, there were twenty-five churches on Franklin Road alone.

In time, I would learn how little I knew and how wrong I was. I didn't consider Nashville a place to waken a sleeping giant. I wouldn't understand for a good long while, but in waiting on God for a simple apartment, he was showing me I had to wait on his timing for *everything*.

121

We arrived in Nashville on a sweltering Monday in August. Harried as it was, the drive was like a kiss from the Father. "Keep going," he whispered in love. "It's new again, yet exactly what I've planned." In the eleventh hour, he provided an apartment in the Nashville suburb of Franklin, so we began the transition to a new city, new friends, and new schools. The first night we slept in a friend's guest room. It was our final night of living between cities, between seasons, between homes.

The next day, after ushering the kids off to school, we met our Q teammates at our new apartment. We'd all relocated the same week from different places—Manhattan, Brooklyn, Atlanta, Michigan, and Connecticut—and were comrades in this new adventure. Mamas and babies and toddlers and tweens, we embarked on making this new ground home. With generous and cheerful hearts, the team helped us unload the U-Haul. Their smiles were a reminder that we were all in this together.

Over the course of the morning, I received multiple texts from local friends offering to bring coffee, arrange the living room, set up the kitchen, entertain the kids, or bring a hot meal. We were in the South again, and I felt it. My eyes welled throughout the day in response to their thoughtfulness. Our friends worked quickly, setting up the beds, couch, and table in under an hour. We packed light, the familiarity of sharing 1,100 square feet in a Manhattan apartment still fresh. By dinner our closets were filled and our cabinets were organized, much faster than planned.

The next order of business was finding food, a perfect excuse for me to sneak away alone. I pulled into a neighborhood grocery store and walked the aisles in a trance, taking twenty-five minutes just to find napkins. I was in a fog of sorts, but somehow I filled the cart. I paid, loaded the groceries into the van, and drove home in the dark as sadness settled over me.

Had we really done this?

Despite its proximity to Nashville, Franklin felt like Mayberry—adorable yet foreign. I'd fought so hard to love New York City when we first moved there, and that labor of love wasn't going to die quickly. I mentally compared this moving day with the day we unloaded our truck onto the Upper East Side. Moving felt like a beginning on that day, but today it felt like an ending. If only I could hang on. Why was I always the last to adjust? Why was letting go so difficult?

During the weeks that followed, I watched as Gabe and the children flourished. But me, I drove my minivan like a martyr. To the grocery store, to carpool, to the gym, declaring under my breath that this move would be great for everyone but me. I would swipe at a stubborn tear when it welled to the point of falling. I read old journal entries to keep my New York memories fresh. I missed my morning runs in Central Park: the pretzel carts, the curtness of New Yorkers, the straightforward edge of even the pigeons. I thought I might be the most reserved person in all of Tennessee, because everyone in Franklin was so friendly, and they *meant* it.

One Tuesday morning, six weeks into my belabored pity party, I was having breakfast with a new friend when she said, "Perhaps God has called you to something, and he's holding it off for a reason." Tears began streaming from my eyes.

What is the reason for these tears, I wondered. As I finished my coffee, I pondered her question, and the answer came:

You cannot see the unknown until you release the known.

It hit me; I needed to *let go* of New York.

So much of my identity had rooted itself there. Manhattan was not merely about real estate or straightforward people. The city was my place of rescue and healing. My sadness wasn't as much about our move to Franklin as it was about the loss of New York and what it represented to me. I fell in love with our life there, and feared this move meant my season of intimacy with God would draw to a close. I was grieving the loss of the place where I was shaped and transformed. I believed God could never be more real to me than on the floorboards of my tiny box of windows in the sky. But how could I experience the unfolding of a new season if I was unwilling to release the old one?

I sat in my van in the parking lot and confessed through my tears:

I'm sorry I've been holding on to what I know. I haven't trusted your guiding or provision. I keep running back to what is familiar instead of opening my heart to a new city and new people. I've grown impatient in the waiting, the unknown. Then I turn around and blame you like you made a mistake. Help me. Forgive me. Teach me how to wait with open hands for a new everything, once again.

124

I've been a runner all of my life—literally and figuratively. Fight or flight has been my *modus operandi*. During our first decade of marriage, my method of conflict resolution with Gabe entailed spewing words or storming out. Thanks to marriage books and loads of grace, we've walked the long, hard road toward learning how to do healthy conflict resolution. Yet the work of healing is never finished, and there are always more areas of our lives that need to be set free. The more I dig, the more bondage I've discovered.

In the early days of our transition to Tennessee, I realized I was not waiting on God; I was in bondage to the tyranny of the now. Isaiah 30:15, 18 says, "In repentance and rest is your salvation, in quietness and trust is your strength, but you would have none of it . . . Yet the Lord longs to be gracious to you; therefore he will rise up to show you compassion. For the Lord is a God of justice. Blessed are all who wait for him!"

I wanted none of it. Not repentance and rest, not quietness and trust—just let me run back to New York City! I thrashed against the work of God, clamoring to know the answers to my questions immediately. All I saw was scarcity, because I was not seeing the transition, the waiting as gifts from God. But his promise is clear—as we wait on him, we discover we are enriched. The waiting is for our salvation, for our good.

Paul knew this too. He told the Corinthians, "I always thank my God for you because of his grace given you in Christ Jesus. For in him you have been enriched in every way—with all kinds of speech and with all knowledge . . . Therefore you do not lack any spiritual gift as you eagerly wait for our Lord Jesus Christ to be revealed."[3]

In other words, *we do not lack as we wait.* Looking back, I see it now: God was gracious and compassionate, gently offering me the time I needed to release New York and wait on him to show me his purposes.

In our waiting, God is working.

Have you ever felt deep in your bones God has a plan "exceedingly abundantly above all that [you] ask or think"?[4] Do you ever "become weary in doing good"?[5] Perhaps you have heard something specific from God. He's awakened you to your passions and talents; he's given you a vision for how you can run fast and free in your lane, but for whatever reason, it's not happening. Doors are not opening, and so you grow impatient.

The fires of passion and zeal burn quickly, but start to fade when we don't see evidence of God's provision and blessing immediately. When things don't happen as we expect—when God doesn't act the way we think he will—we begin to question and doubt everything.

Did we hear correctly?

Did we get it wrong?

We expect immediate parting of the seas, removal of obstacles, and opening of doors, yet Scripture shows us that God often calls his children to periods of waiting. Consider David and how he was anointed king of Israel, only to be sent back to tend his family's sheep. God clearly revealed that he chose David to be king, yet the pregnancy of his anointing lasted years. As David waited, the Lord made him ready. Then in due season, when the giant Goliath threatened the entire nation, God told David, *It's time.* The Lord prepared David to stand against and defeat his enemy. The waiting strengthened David to lead in that moment. That's how many promises of the Bible are laid out.

There's a revealing, followed by a period of waiting.

The writer of Hebrews tells the church, "Do not cast away your confidence, [church], which has great reward. For you have need of endurance, so that after you have done the will of God, you may receive the promise."[6]

The life of the believer hangs in the balance between the now and the not yet. We know the hope—that the kingdom would come on earth as it is in heaven—but we live in the waiting. In the same way, we can know the call of God on our lives and feel anxious to get to it, but God sometimes calls us to wait as he refines us, as he shows himself to be our redeemer, rescuer, and healer. We must confess that his timing is best, and trust and declare that the waiting will bring us into a place of readiness.

Perhaps you are waiting in hope that a broken relationship will be repaired. Maybe you are waiting for the return of a loved one with whom you've lost touch. Perhaps you've held off on divorce, hoping for the restoration of your marriage. Maybe you're waiting for physical healing.

You straddle promise and doubt, feebly holding onto the hope of promise. Keep holding on. You may not know the outcome, but you can rest in the tension of the waiting. It's in the tension that the music is made. Remember the song of the psalmist, "How long, LORD?"[7]

When will the supernatural meet the natural?

When will you show up in all your glory and swoop the broken-hearted into your palm? When will you fly by and tuck us in your mighty wings?[8] We sit on the precipice of promise, and the posture of waiting requires ultimate surrender of the human will. No matter how much we want to change things or rush them, we cannot. It is out of our hands.

Here, in the waiting, God gently responds:

I am working on your behalf even now.

In the tension I hold you.

In the waiting, I walk with you.

In the not-yet, I carry you.

Rest here, in green pastures, by streams of living water.

In this place of utter safety and comfort.

Let me shelter you with the wing of my mighty hand.

Let me flood you with complete safety.

I see you and I will cover you. I will hold you fast.

There will come a moment in your waiting when God says, "It's time." There is a season for each of us, where we will reap if we do not faint. He shows us the way. We need grace and wisdom to sit in the places prepared for us, because we've been given an anointing to be revealed in time. God has something in store for you and only you. Waiting is a critical part of your anointing. It prepares you, strengthens you, equips and trains you to step up when the moment comes.

When I at last released New York, my vitality slowly returned. I had new hope, new optimism, and new expectancy. I was waking up to why God sometimes holds things off. How could I wait in hope for the future while I clung to what was behind me? Until I was ready to let go of the past, God was content to let me wait.

Jesus wanted my all; he wanted my surrender. I was about to learn what that meant.

Becoming Free

1. Are you waiting for a job situation to resolve, marriage wounds to heal, or a child to come home? Have you grown weary in the waiting? List the areas in which you are tired of waiting.

2. Can you recognize the ways in which God is equipping you, even in this waiting? Ask him to show you the ways, and make a list.

3. Are there times the waiting makes you want to revert to what you already know, even though God has given you a glimpse of something yet to happen? If so, feel free to confess your struggle in prayer or in a journal. He can handle it and may even reveal more insight after your confession.

4. Surrender to God's timing with this prayer: *Jesus, I know you love me and have called me for a purpose. Teach me to wait as you equip me for that purpose. I trust you.*

9

Free to Rest

> *Rest time is not waste time.*
> *It is economy to gather fresh strength . . .*
> *It is wisdom to take occasional furlough.*
> *In the long run, we shall do more by sometimes doing less.*
>
> **CHARLES SPURGEON**[1]

WHEN MY GRIEF OVER LOSING New York lifted, the tears stopped. I ventured out to find a new normal. Autumn rolled in, and our Tennessee morning commute was awash with yellows, oranges, and reds. I hopped from our van most days to capture at least one shot through my camera lens. Creation had a freeing effect on me; its beauty grabbed my breath and halted my tracks.

It turned out God knew I needed a soft landing, and our new hometown offered subtle reminders of the things we enjoyed most about New York City. Our townhouse was across the street from a public farm where our family walked many evenings at dusk. Gabe, Cade, and I dropped the poodles at the dog park and circled the pond while the younger kids biked the trails. It wasn't the Hudson River, but the sight of the sun bouncing off the water's surface in the day's final moments felt as glorious as the sunsets I'd experienced in New York. What's more, our little living room mirrored the one in our glass house in the Manhattan sky.

God doesn't miss a detail. How could I have doubted him?

We were even able to maintain some of the pedestrian lifestyle we'd grown to love. In TriBeCa, our kids walked to their school a block away, we walked two blocks east to church, and the grocery store was two minutes from our front door. This pedestrian pace cleared my head; in fact, when stuck in the midst of a writing project, I'd stop working and walk when my sentences became sluggish.

In Franklin, I held onto that pace. We walked to the farmers market most Saturday mornings, chasing down hot apple cider donuts with fruit smoothies, then loading up on raw veggies to ease the sugar guilt. Even our new Q offices were positioned just off Main Street in our new, all-American downtown. For lunch each day, we could stroll out for pastries or paleo, whatever our whim.

When we arrived in Franklin, I began hearing a refrain. Friends would comment in passing or look me square in the eye and say, *"You are entering a season of rest."* But I did not want to rest.

If you asked me, it seemed pretty clear I'd only begun to run the race referenced in Hebrews 12:1. There was work to be done—people to be ministered to, friends to be encouraged, loved ones to be set free! *Rest is not something a runner wants to hear about.* Leaving behind the fast pace of the city, I felt like I'd been benched, or worse, tripped in my lane while the rest of the runners went whizzing by.

Then one of my dearest friends and neighbors from New York called to check in on how I was adjusting. Rebekah, a mother of three who shared my name down to the k-a-h, had witnessed my ups and downs firsthand. She was the first New Yorker who welcomed me into her home, and helped me find my footing once we settled in. The two of us have matching brass angel Christmas ornaments with a dangling bell and our names etched on the side, circa early 1980s. In addition to our names and our mamas' tastes in Christmas decorations, Rebekah and I share in the fight for sustained mental health. We are kindred spirits who vacillate between living well and living hollow, and we agree we don't want the latter.

During our call Rebekah couldn't stop talking about a book she was reading—*The Artist's Way* by Julia Cameron. She said the book encourages creatives to establish a daily rhythm of writing, which she was doing, and it was strengthening her heart. She thought it might inspire mine, too. I decided to join in the rhythm. I picked up a copy of the book and immediately started reading.

Cameron proposes that our natural ego defenses are down and we are most in tune with our subconscious for the first forty minutes after we wake up. She recommends we spend those early moments journaling, and calls this daily rhythm Morning Pages. This was a big change for me. I usually dedicate those forty minutes to a mental list of tasks, stressing about what I forgot the day prior, wondering why I can't measure up.

Cameron's words inspired me: "We should write because it is human nature to write. We should write because writing is a powerful form of prayer and meditation. We should write, above all, because we are writers whether we call ourselves writers or not."[2] I was hooked. Her words would radically alter my daily experience.

The next morning I rolled out of bed, brewed coffee, lit a candle, and put pen to paper. This daily practice—pajama practice, I soon called it—was the first time I'd tried journaling since a sporadic attempt during college. And it was an awkward reentry. In college, I felt an obligation to offer every linear detail to the journal gods, like a fact sheet to track my activities with an occasional "aha moment" thrown in. But that wasn't the point, was it? In my Morning Pages, I took a different approach. The pages beckoned me to return as an old friend, to let down my guard and pick up where I'd left off a couple decades prior, as if I'd simply lost power mid-sentence.

I began again and scratched these words:

When I stray from reflection, life strays away from me.

I become restless and fragmented, busy and insecure.

I compare, compete, and strive. My best parts become my worst parts.

Then I remember Jesus' final promise to make all things new.

Morning Pages, for me, are a ritual of redemption.

For the first time since I could remember, I was able to write *freely*, unconcerned about how what I wrote might sound to someone else or whether it might be uncovered a century later by curious grandchildren. Morning Pages are the cheapest kind of therapy, I tell you. Daily, the words landed with fluid ink against the crisp paper. Letters marched their way in neat rows across the pages of my journal, and I found myself engaged in an ongoing conversation with God. This early morning exercise was reclaiming my soul.

What I found in these morning conversations was startling.

There were places where I was still held captive.

Through these pages, I dug deep and found strongholds that needed to be released and confessed. I poured out my heart, moving from lament to exuberance in a single hour. Some days dawned with confused pleas as I wondered what God was up to in this world. Others opened with questions about how God could possibly love us so deeply. No matter the topic, the Lord met me in the silence with promises like manna in the wilderness.

My dialogue with God deepened over the ensuing months. Some entries filled three pages (the number suggested by Cameron), yet others filled eight or more. There was something breathtaking about writing in a hushed house before dawn, when no one hears and no one sees except the One who knows us best, who knits us back together when we are broken. The words brought insights as old, forgotten memories surfaced. It was a workout of the mind. In my journaling I'd found a haven where I could reflect and rest, plan and prepare, renew and remind myself to keep moving forward one day at a time.

One morning, I wrote these words, God's whispers to my heart: *Initiate nothing. Watch what I can do.*

It was clear. God was calling me to rest. Unsure why I needed a reprieve—it seemed I'd only just begun to run in my calling—I reluctantly took off my running shoes.

Sometimes it takes a stripping away of what we know in order for us to be willing to stop and learn. Little did I know I was about to enter a long season of solitude and stillness. I later called it Kitchen Seminary, because in this season I began to understand more of God's story.

A friend gave me a *Chronological Life Application Study Bible*, which has Scripture arranged so events appear in the order they occurred, divided into ten eras of biblical history. The books intermingle to help you understand how each story actually unfolded. I'm a context junkie, always hungry for the *why* behind the *what*, so I began to inhale the grand story of God with new hunger. I wanted to understand all of it, from beginning to end.

During this period my lifelong friend Trina came to visit. She brought me *Abiding in Christ* by Andrew Murray, a consequential book written in 1895. (I like to read books by dead people; they cut through the noise of today.) It was a timely love letter on the relationship between the Vine (Jesus) and the branch (the believer). Between sips of coffee and blueberry scones, I devoured it.

I wouldn't have asked for it, but the Lord awakened me at four a.m. every day for four weeks straight so I could read. I savored every page; it became dog-eared, the text inside underlined, circled, and highlighted, with exclamation points filling the margins. As I studied, I wrote my own nuggets of truth and wisdom in my journal. As the winter unfolded, one message rang loud and clear:

Stop performing for love.

Why was I still struggling to let go of this particular stronghold and walk in freedom? Somewhere deep down, I still believed you had to "Put your head down and work hard! There's a harvest, go get it!" Somehow I believed if I wasn't hustling, striving, constantly posting on social media, and leveraging every possible opportunity to make Christ known, I was not a super-Christian. And super-Christians are the ones who change the world. Right?

In the quiet I heard God whisper the opposite:

> "Are you tired? Worn out? Burned out on religion? Come to me, [Rebekah]. Get away with me and you'll recover your life. I'll show you how to take a real rest. Walk with me and work with me—watch how I do it."[3]

I need you to take a rest.

In other words, I didn't need to work harder or fight more. I didn't need to hustle or strive. I didn't have to win any journaling competitions, didn't need to record every waking minute of every day. I confessed right then and there:

Jesus, I'm exhausted. Running around in circles, trying to keep up with things I've imposed upon myself in order to make others happy. Please show me how to recover my life. Help me initiate nothing, but to come close in the dark hours of the early morning. Make the work light.

I trusted Jesus would show me what was next. I released my plans for serving him and took the vow to initiate nothing. I would rest. I would wait to see what he unfolded. I did not need to figure it all out on my own. He could be trusted. When it was time, he would take my hand and say, "This is the way; walk in it."[4]

A few months later, the posture of rest was making more sense. Seasons of heavy commitments had drawn to a close, making room for newfound joys to spring forth. One of these delights was an opportunity to study under the teaching of a rabbinical guide in Israel with a small group of dear friends. For a week we journeyed through many places in Scripture: the Pool of Bethesda, Jacob's Well, the Jordan River, Shiloh, the Cave of Adullam, Capernaum, the Holy City, the Garden Tomb, and more.

At the end of a full week of walking in the footsteps of Jesus, we were treated to a final lazy afternoon during Shabbat (the Jewish Sabbath). We'd been staying at a gorgeous kibbutz all week, inspired by the garden and the community that lived and worked there, overlooking the Emmaus road.

This particular afternoon, I went for a stroll alone. As I made my way down the dirt path that overlooked a vineyard, an eastern wind whirled up fast and furious. I stopped in my tracks, my imagination running wild, as if Jesus were about to stroll around the bend to offer me a bear hug. (A girl can dream, yes?) Moments later my eyes landed on a branch dangling in front of me; I was standing beneath a grape arbor canopied with vines.

Upon looking closer, I noticed a tiny leaf, torn almost in two. At the bottom of the leaf, a green vine had wrapped itself in a ball around the torn part, binding the tear and holding the leaf closely against itself. I choked up. This was a picture I wouldn't soon forget. During the first years in New York, I had described myself as "untethered," flailing and fluttering like that torn leaf. Instantly I understood the metaphor and what the true Vine had been doing in me.

I ran to gather the rest of my group, to show them this gift of analogy. Our guide, Arie, joined us with bright eyes, his zeal for a teachable moment palpable. He shared that whenever a vine touches something, its nature is to begin wrapping itself around the object, making them one.

For a year I'd been marinating in my season of resting and abiding, learning how this Vine and branch relationship worked. Murray's words resurfaced in my mind:

> "Wandering one, as it was Jesus who drew you when he said 'Come,' so it is Jesus who keeps you when he says, 'Abide.' The grace to come and the grace to abide are both from him alone. That word *come*, heard, meditated on, accepted, was the chord of love to draw you close; the word *abide* is the band with which he holds you fast and binds you to himself."[5]

The apostle Paul wrote in his letter to the church in Philippi, "I press on to take hold of that for which Christ Jesus took hold of me."[6] Union with Christ is prompted by Christ humself.

The nature of the vine is to wrap around whatever it encounters and to make them one.

When I stopped running, Jesus drew near. In the midst of my rest, the Vine held me close. Morning Pages were my entrance to abiding, and rest gave me permission to remain in him. I'd learned something during those months that I'd hold tightly forever:

God cares more about our presence than our performance.

I'd always thought my closeness with Jesus was dependent on me. Consequently, I was an Energizer bunny for him. But Jesus' love draws us in for one thing: to come into his presence and his rest, to stop working and doing and striving, to remain in him. That's it.

How many of us could use a little soul rest? When we do come, the Vine pulls us close and tethers us to himself. There is no limit to the life flowing from the Vine to the branch.

The greatness doesn't stop there. This tethering becomes our provision, meaning all the nutrients of heaven are offered to us right now, to renew us and bring us back to life. Everything the Vine possesses belongs to the branches. Jesus gives us everything we need to push back the darkness.[7] He gently binds us to himself. When we rest in him, when we abide in him, he brings us into a fruit-producing life that feeds and nourishes others. Fruit never grows from our efforts alone; it grows according to the measure we let God grow it in us. Without the Vine, the branch can do nothing. Without the branch, the Vine will not produce. As Murray puts it, "Such is the wonderful condescension of the grace of Jesus, just as his people are dependent on him, he has made himself dependent on them."[8]

God chooses us, and we choose him. God blesses us, and we bless him. But this exchange cannot happen unless we first learn to rest and abide in him. If we are not free to rest, we will either burn out or the work will be about our agenda, not God's. In a society of to-dos and goals and ambitions, the Father asks us to rest *assured*. He wants us to stop trying so hard to matter.

What a beautiful relief! The old covenant was about what we bring to *him*: our annual offering, our covering of sin to become restored with God. The new covenant is all about what Jesus brings to *us*: his offering, his blood to forgive our sins, and his righteousness credited to us, making us right with God.

God's got this. He's done the work, and we are free to rest. May we stop striving and rest in the grip of the Vine's loving kindness.

Becoming Free

1. Are you tired? Worn out? So many of us run, run, run, finding ourselves constantly busy. What are some ways you keep yourself busy? Confess these things, listing them before God. Ask him to show you how to recover your life.

2. When is the last time you really rested? How might you carve out daily time for quiet, for unplugging from media, for rest?

3. Determine some areas of busyness you could do without. List some places you could pull back so that you could live into a more restful pace.

4. Pray this prayer: *Lord, teach me how to rest. Teach me how to pull back from activity so that I can lean into you. Show me how to encounter "rest for my soul."*

10

Free to
Grieve

I do not understand why others
are able to find new life
in the midst of a living death,
though I am one of them.
PARKER PALMER[1]

*W*HEN YOU ASK GOD to set you free, to show you the areas where you are or have been in bondage, he will. I knelt in prayer in my living room and prayed, *Show me the places you've already set me free, places I might not have recognized.* There came a flood of emotions pushing against my chest walls, rising up in my throat, welling in my eyes.

Do you remember the first time you grieved? he asked. *There was a freedom there.* His whisper immediately evoked memories from fifteen years earlier.

On February 1, 2001, I was thirty-nine weeks pregnant. I waddled into my obstetrician's office for a final, routine checkup. Believing my belly had stopped growing, I asked the nurse, "Do you ever do ultrasounds at the end?"

"Not unless you are unusually large or small," she said.

At that point my face was swollen more than my belly, so I said, "Well, I'm not unusually *large*."

I hoisted myself up on the table, and she measured my tummy. Thirty-five centimeters. I should have measured thirty-nine centimeters to match my thirty-nine weeks. It was enough of a deficit to warrant another ultrasound.

I shuffled to radiology, where the technician slathered my belly with goo and slid the scope around and around over the top. We could hear the baby's heartbeat, audible but faint. She studied the screen for a while, silent. I waited. Finally, she responded, "I need to check this out further. I'm not the best at reading this; let's get another technician to take a look."

I waited for a bit, and then the doctor came in and said, "I'm going to go ahead and send you to the hospital for a level-two ultrasound. The radiology specialists are more skilled at seeing everything."

I sensed something was wrong, so before leaving I asked the technician, "Should we go ahead and schedule next week's checkup?" I was testing her.

Her response confirmed my fear. "Let's wait and see what we find out," she said.

As I left the office, I dialed the mister with shaking hands.

"Babe," I said, my voice quavering, "You need to get to the hospital right now." Just saying the words brought on a tremor, but I did my best to hold it back.

The fifteen-minute drive to the Baby Factory—that's what we called

Northside Hospital in Atlanta—felt like an infinity. Gabe met me in the waiting room, where the clock crawled for another hour. Hurry up and wait. My brain was everywhere, wanting to know what was going on with our baby. A nurse finally called us back and set me up for the ultrasound. When the doctor came in, he looked at the screen for a mere thirty seconds and said, "Your baby is 4.9 pounds, full term. You have lost all your fluid. He is failing to thrive and not growing anymore. You need to have this baby today."

Off I went to labor and delivery, where I was given an epidural and a heart monitor was strapped to my belly. I'm no doctor, but I can follow a rhythm, and as I listened to the cadence of our baby's heart, it was clearly slowing. When I realized his heart rate had dropped into the sixties, the mama bear in me finally found her voice.

"This baby is coming out *now*," I said. "Give me the drugs." Twenty minutes later I was being rolled into the operating room for a C-section, where I was given another epidural.

Cade Christian Lyons was out in ten minutes flat. By then the second epidural kicked in, and my entire body went numb, including my tongue, my arms, and even my lungs. I panicked.

I'm dying, I thought. *I'll die right here on this table while everyone is working with Cade.* And then, *Wait. I'm totally overreacting. There's no reason to be negative and speak that into existence.* A few more seconds passed.

Just in case I'm dying, I should probably tell someone. After all, I'm on an operating room table. It only seems right.

I slurred, "I'm dyyyyyyying." And my sweet husband, who is very, very bright, asked the doctor, "Is this normal?" The doctor rushed over, looked into my eyes, and told me, "If you stop breathing, we can breathe for you." Not quite the reassurance I was hoping for. If only I could lift my middle finger.

Six hours later, at one a.m., I was still sleeping off the meds, with Gabe dozing on a cot a foot away. Cade was nowhere in sight. The door opened and I saw a man's silhouette in the hallway, fluorescent light illuminating his frame from behind—but this was no angel. The doctor spoke from the threshold, telling us he'd been studying Cade in the transition nursery.

"We see signs of Down syndrome in your baby," he said. "I want to have a geneticist run tests so we can be certain."

Both dumbfounded, Gabe and I made eye contact, then looked back at the doctor with concern as Gabe rattled off a few basic questions: *What does this mean? When can we hold him? How did this happen?* The doctor shrugged and said we could talk about it in the morning. Without an ounce of emotion left, I fell back on the pillows and into sleep. Perhaps drugs are good for moments like that.

The next morning I hoisted my body into a wheelchair (I still had no feeling in my legs), and Gabe and I took the elevator one floor down to the Neonatal Intensive Care Unit. There, I saw my son for the very first time—my sweet, towheaded boy, sleeping soundly in an acrylic box with IVs in his arms and an oxygen tube under his nose. Wires were everywhere. Still, he looked peaceful. I stuck my hand into the side opening, just to feel his skin. It was soft, flawless. As we gazed at our son, a geneticist explained which of Cade's features were common indicators of Down syndrome. It would be several days before lab results could confirm if our son had an extra Chromosome 21.

For five days I held out hope. After all, Cade didn't have a heart defect, and half of Down syndrome kids do, so maybe Mr. Geneticist Doctor was wrong. I attempted to breastfeed, but Cade couldn't latch on, his tongue too weak to nurse. As we waited for news, I pumped like crazy. Meanwhile, Gabe and I also fed Cade formula from a medicine dropper every three hours, as the doctors felt this would accelerate his weight gain. Friends and family—even strangers—flooded us with kindness, sending flowers, balloons, prayers, emails, and cards. We were suddenly *that* family.

I remained at the hospital for the next three days, but had to leave when my insurance coverage ran out. I sobbed as Gabe wheeled me, empty-armed, to our car. Cade would have to remain in the hospital until he weighed five pounds.

The next morning, I woke early and jumped in the shower, ready to head back to the NICU. I'd been without Cade for almost eight hours, and it was killing me. The phone rang, and I heard Gabe answer. I knew it was the doctor calling with the lab results. Sixty seconds crawled by. Gabe cracked open the shower door. Seeing the look on his face, I collapsed.

There will never be words to describe the pain I felt at that moment. I had no idea I was capable of such grief, yet there I was, wailing. I could not shed the anguish fast enough.

Something died in me that day: the controlled plan for my "perfect" life. In return, something was born that day: surrender to an uncharted and forever-changing path. As my body slowly emptied of tears, I noticed something. I was weeping in both body and spirit, my body trembling beyond control, yet a transfer was happening. Jesus was taking my pain upon himself. He'd done the same on the cross, for all of us.

Gabe and I drove to the hospital in silence. I realized I didn't know a single person with Down syndrome. I was ashamed I'd overlooked this community, a sorority of mothers whose children had Down syndrome—a sorority to which I now belonged.

We walked into the NICU, and as I swept up Cade in my arms, his eyes made contact with mine as if to say, "Will you love me for me? Not for what I can do or accomplish? Not for the milestones I can meet so you feel like a good mom?"

The performer in me melted. Already those sky blue eyes were reminding me that God doesn't measure worth in terms of ability, but in terms of identity. We're sons and daughters, adopted into the family of God, grafted onto the vine of Jesus, heirs to a throne. This understanding was a grace, a God-given lease of unconditional love upon my entrance to motherhood at age twenty-six. My grief, just a few hours old, was already bringing me comfort.

I think about other times when I was free to grieve. I remember when, less than two years after Cade's birth, one of our dearest friends and coworkers, Adam, suffered a heart attack at age twenty-seven. The night before, we were out together as couples, eating ribs and celebrating another friend's birthday. Gabe was in the same building when Adam fell the next afternoon. He and another friend arrived right away and frantically tried to administer CPR. When I got the call, I prayed for an hour on the floor in our living room, weeping for Adam, his wife, Lisa, and their seven-month-old daughter, Arden. Adam died that day, and four days later, fifteen hundred of us responded with worship at his funeral. We knew the Lord heard us, and wept with us. He comforted us.

When tears flooded my pillow those first two years in NYC, I found comfort in the words of Psalm 30:5 (paraphrased here): There may be pain in the night, but joy comes in the morning. This verse has proven to be true over and over again. I like to think of it like this: There will be pain in the night, but joy comes in the *mourning*. It's the mourning process that releases our pain, I think.

Some people have been taught that tears mean you are feeling sorry for yourself. They believe the Christian life makes no room for sadness, gives no permission for grief, allows no time for lament. This kind of mental toughness might seem like the best approach for immediate survival, but unexpressed grief can become a bitterness that chokes us.

If we cannot grieve, we cannot be comforted.[2]

When we dull our pain, we dull our joy. When we numb our lows, we numb our highs.

Jesus has a different perspective on grief. He never lacked emotion or expression. Isaiah 53:3 says, "Jesus was a man of sorrows, acquainted with grief." His most passionate sermon—the Beatitudes in the Sermon on the Mount—began with "Blessed are those that mourn, for they will be comforted."[3]

Jesus wept with his dear friends Mary and Martha when their brother, Lazarus, died. "When Jesus saw her weeping, and the Jews who had come along with her also weeping, he was deeply moved in spirit, and troubled.' Where have you laid him?' he asked. 'Come and see, Lord,' they replied. Jesus wept."[4] The Greek word for wept here is *dakruo,* which means "to lament, to mourn, specifically for the dead." Jesus was free to grieve! He was filled with empathy for his friends and shared in their tears. He felt *with* them and *for* them in their sadness. Perhaps he mourned the loss of his friend, even though he knew he would raise Lazarus from the dead.[5]

Jesus also wept loudly for the fate of his beloved Jerusalem. "As he approached Jerusalem and saw the city, he wept over it and said, 'If you, even you, had only known on this day what would bring you peace—but now it is hidden from your eyes.'"[6] The Greek word for wept here is *klaio,* which means "weep, cry aloud . . . the whole personality is involved, as it is in the case of a crying child."[7]

And when he was in the garden that final evening before he was arrested, Jesus wept for himself. "He took Peter and Zebedee's two sons, James and John, and he became anguished and distressed. He told them, 'My soul is crushed with grief to the point of death. Stay here and keep watch with me.'"[8]

Jesus wept from empathy, from disappointment, from pain. He mourned, and when he was finished mourning, he surrendered to the work of God—work that brought great freedom to all of us.

Sooner or later, most of us will experience a moment when everything in our lives changes. When we realize life doesn't look the way we expected it to. Or what we dreamed it would be. Suddenly we are faced with a moment of crisis. For Gabe and me, this happened when we learned the news about Cade. For others it is the death of a loved one or news of a terminal illness.

I've grieved with friends who have walked through fear and loss. Loss of love and marriage vows. Loss of sanity and peace. Loss of life, in the womb and out. I've watched those same folks handed dying day grace—when they experience a death of their own will and embrace Jesus' comfort.

When in the middle of a painful season, with no end in sight, we question how long we must wait for rescue. Everything in us wants to run, to escape the pain we are experiencing, to look for ways to become numb when the pain becomes too much to bear. We wonder if God has forsaken us. But God responds differently, "Turn your face to me. Focus on me, because I have exceeding and abundant plans above all you could ever ask or think." Dare we believe it?

The dysfunction of this world will be tangible, again and again. We cannot escape it—although we desperately try.

Tears confess our need for comfort. Lament is a different kind of confession, one beyond words. It's where the Spirit confesses for us, with groans we can't express. "In the same way, the Spirit helps us in our weakness. For we do not know how we ought to pray, but the Spirit Himself intercedes for us with groans too deep for words."[9]

I believe grief is our most powerful confession, because it cracks our hearts wide open. The Spirit prays for what we need in that moment, in ways we can't imagine. This kind of physical expression of confession keeps our hearts clean. Tears are a soul-cleansing way to release any seeds of bitterness. Deep grief can take us to new depths of brokenness and surrender. In the depths of grief we realize mourning brings the comfort of God, and above all, God is waiting to rescue us in our darkest hour.

Isn't that what faith is all about—trusting God is working something beautiful and beyond our wildest imagination? Jesus, in the flesh, joined our sufferings in life and death. But the third morning after his death, at dawn, he gave us an example of exceeding abundance. A promise of hope for all who believe.

Richard Rohr speaks of humanity's longing for wholeness in his book, *Falling Upward*. He points out that we long for a home where wrong is made right, where sickness takes flight. He observes that we long for redemption, where death is raised to life. "Wouldn't it make sense that God would plant in us a desire for what God already wants to give us? I am sure of it." Rohr writes. "There is an inherent and desirous dissatisfaction that both sends and draws us forward, and it comes from our original and radical union with God. There is a God sized hole in all of us, waiting to be filled."[10] But here's the truth I've found: we only find that wholeness, that unity, when we allow ourselves to mourn the death of our worldly expectations.

Today, I can attest that Cade is the barometer of wholeness in our home. He brings peace, joy, and freedom to everyone in our family. He grins from ear to ear when we demonstrate love, and his tears roll slowly when we act selfish. I've experienced more peace with Cade than with anyone else. I've experienced more joy with Cade than with anyone else. Although I now know the blessing he is, there was a time for grieving the loss of what I imagined.

I'll admit, I'm a sensitive girl. Tears come easily. I've always felt permission to cry, but it wasn't until I learned about Cade's diagnosis that I understood God was teaching me a kind of freedom offered through grief, a freedom that comes from releasing our expectations and expressing sadness over our losses. Somehow, when I'm faithful to the grieving process, when I give in to mourning, I find great freedom on the other side. I find my sole remedy in Christ. I find the God shaped hole is filled a little more.

Every time we express grief, we allow Jesus to absorb our pain. When we live out the freedom we have been given to grieve, Jesus takes our grief upon himself and replaces it with comfort. What a precious gift.

Becoming Free

1. So many of us stuff our emotions, bottle up our tears. Are there circumstances in your life that you haven't fully grieved? Consider the loss of loved ones or the death of expectations.

2. Consider finding a quiet place where others will not worry about you if you give in to grief. Confess to God your desire to grieve. Ask him to teach you how to give in to grief. Spend time feeling the emotions of your grief.

3. Ask God to comfort you, even in your mourning.

4. If your grief is too weighty, even in the presence of God, consider seeking out a professional therapist or counselor. Sometimes God uses others to bring his people into his comfort and rest.

11

Free to Be Weak

The weaker we feel, the harder we lean.
The harder we lean, the stronger we grow spiritually,
even while our bodies waste away.

J.I. PACKER

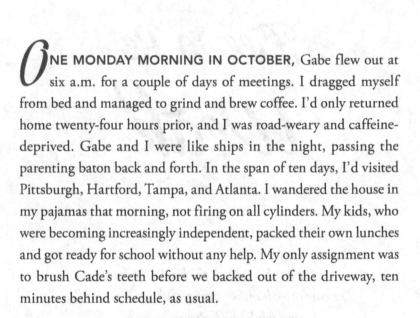

ONE MONDAY MORNING IN OCTOBER, Gabe flew out at six a.m. for a couple of days of meetings. I dragged myself from bed and managed to grind and brew coffee. I'd only returned home twenty-four hours prior, and I was road-weary and caffeine-deprived. Gabe and I were like ships in the night, passing the parenting baton back and forth. In the span of ten days, I'd visited Pittsburgh, Hartford, Tampa, and Atlanta. I wandered the house in my pajamas that morning, not firing on all cylinders. My kids, who were becoming increasingly independent, packed their own lunches and got ready for school without any help. My only assignment was to brush Cade's teeth before we backed out of the driveway, ten minutes behind schedule, as usual.

All was calm for a minute, then the questions ensued. *Who will help Cade get the right shoe on the right foot? Who gets to pick the movie for the morning ride? Who gets to sit in the front seat of the minivan after school? Why is Mom always looking at her phone? Can we have a slumber party on Friday?* I blindly nodded—or did I?—as I half listened, half ran from the barrage of questions, including my own: *Why is the music so loud? Why are my children so loud? Why is every question an opportunity for an argument?*

We pulled into the school drop-off lane, and I tried to salvage our final seconds.

"Hey, guys. Sorry about the tension this morning," I said. "I love you." It was a feeble attempt at repair, and it was too little, too late. I pulled away from the school as regrets began to circle my mind in the quiet.

I felt I was not enough. I drove home as if in a trance. I entered the house, surveying it for the first time in days. The silence was deafening. In the sink was a tower of food-crusted dishes. I grabbed the plate on the top of the stack, began to scrub, and the tower crumbled, shattering a glass beneath its shifting weight. I wondered, *How fragile are these dishes? How fragile am I?*

I left the broken pieces in the sink, walked into the living room, and knelt face down on the oriental rug. *Jesus, help.* I was exhausted. I loved teaching, but I needed to slow down. I would come home from a trip just long enough to do laundry and restock the fridge before leaving again. The pace was wearing me out.

Each speaking engagement brought new encounters with new people, many of whom were like cracked glasses themselves, shattering or ready to shatter. Out on the front lines, I prayed with anyone who shared their story and asked for prayer. One woman told me she asks men to call her a whore as they ravage her. I asked her when the abuse began. She said as long as she remembered. A college girl confessed she'd made two suicide attempts in the past eight years. She was struggling with suicidal thoughts again, fighting the darkness that was calling her under. Another described her morning manic episode. She'd been diagnosed with bipolar disorder as a child, and after a season of reprieve, she'd relapsed.

Through a thin veil I saw the darkness of the world, and it was massive. I was not equipped to fight against it. I wasn't strong enough.

" For the Spirit God gave us does not make us timid, but gives us power, love and self-discipline."[1]

From my earliest memories, I repeated these words. I whispered them after nightmares about our house burning to the ground as my sisters and I escaped in our nightgowns. I whispered them when I left for college fifteen hours from home. And I whispered them as Gabe and I rushed Cade to the ER on countless nights during croup attacks. Children with Down syndrome suffer from small airways, and Cade's croup always escalated quickly. With just seconds to spare, we'd throw on sweats and flip-flops, barrel down the stairs, and drive four miles to Northside Hospital.

Each time, I sat in the backseat with Cade in my arms, singing to keep him calm. These ER trips continued month after month, year after year for the next decade. Gabe and I slept intermittently with a video monitor at our bedside, the volume turned as high as it could go, awaiting the next barking gasp. After Pierce and Kennedy were born, we'd leave them in their beds and call the neighbors, who slipped in the back door to wait on the couch until we returned.

It was only the beginning of how Cade stretched us. One early December morning when he was five, Cade left his yogurt container and spoon on the kitchen counter and walked out the side door, down the driveway, and up the street wearing only a diaper. It was twenty-six degrees. He was trying to follow Gabe, who'd left early for a meeting. My blonde boy walked barefoot for half a mile through the neighborhood.

A teenage girl driving by saw our near-naked toddler struggling along in the cold and stopped to help him. He could only utter "Daddy" through his cries. She placed him in her backseat, blasting the heat on his chubby legs. She stopped every car that passed for the next ten minutes in an effort to find someone who could knew him. Our next door neighbor, on her way to run an errand, stopped and immediately recognized Cade. The teenage Good Samaritan insisted on following my neighbor back to my house, Cade in tow. (She was invested and not about to hand Cade over to a stranger.) They pulled into my driveway as I was backing out of the garage to go searching with Pierce and Kennedy. I'd already scoured the block on foot, whispering 2 Timothy 1:7 over and over.

When he was seven, Cade wandered off at the mall. Security found him dancing in the back of Hollister.

When he was nine, he went exploring in Central Park (it was our first week in New York City), where park rangers and a class from Boston College retrieved him in a golf cart.

When he was ten, during the week of Hurricane Irene, Cade disappeared in a water park in the Bahamas. We found him thirty minutes later, at the front of the line for the most popular waterslide, the four-story *Leap of Faith*. It turned out it was the fourth time he'd cut in front of everyone. No one had the heart to turn away his silly grin.

When he was twelve, he took himself shopping in downtown TriBeCa, sneaking from the children's section of Barnes & Noble to the adjacent Bed Bath & Beyond. I found him barefoot in the checkout line, scanning the bar code of a Vitamix. At least my firstborn fugitive was health-conscious.

One Sunday afternoon just before we moved to Franklin, Cade left a party and crossed three streets in Queens by himself. Thanks to the NYPD and friends circling the blocks in their cars, we found him exiting a bar two streets away, Coke in hand. He is never afraid, this firstborn of mine. He has a chronic streak of independence and exploration. The rest of us respond with a chronic streak of panic, a chronic rush of adrenaline.

Over time, the recurring panic and resultant adrenaline rush took their toll on me. Experts say chronic trauma can be more damaging than a single devastating event, because you are never able to relax. The trauma is unrelenting. I felt this my first moments as a mama, when Cade was whisked to the NICU before I even got to hold him. I wore fear like a pair of ankle weights. I endured it until I couldn't anymore, and fear moved in.

I can't explain why fear is so pervasive in our society. I can only speak to the ways my own fear unraveled me and how God was faithful, even in the dark. My panic stemmed from the persistent trauma and physical exhaustion related to caring for a highly unpredictable child. But even though my anxiety was justifiable, that did not negate the damaging impact it had on my soul.

Most of us carry chronic stress for so long we no longer recognize the weight of it. That's why I call it a grace when our bodies rebel. It is God's way of saying, *No more*. Eventually, we can no longer sustain such a life. And what about those who carry the kinds of stress confessed to me during my travels? What about those who are abused, who struggle with bipolar disorder, depression, or suicidal thoughts? What of those who endure the darkest kinds of suffering meted out by humankind?

How many of us try to manage our stress with some method of numbing ourselves? The problem with pain management is exactly that: we are *managing*. What if we are called to acknowledge our pain, to confess our inability to beat it? What if we're called to admit our weakness and declare that only God's strength is sufficient?

God wants us to reveal our weakness—to recognize what traumatizes and exhausts us. He wants us to confess our wounds, our sources of pain and stress, and bring them into the light so he can redeem and transform them with his strength. Have you confessed to him your exhaustion, your fear, your stress? Have you confessed that God wants to display his strength in your weakness?

Mental and emotional healing can take longer than physical healing, because emotional ailments often stay hidden for much longer and therefore have deeper roots. It is hard to heal what has been hidden, and sometimes God calls us to sit in the emotional pain for weeks, months, or even years before the fullness of his healing comes.

I'm often asked, "When you were in the thick of panic attacks and depression, did you ever feel disqualified from ministering to others?" During that season, I wrestled silently. Perhaps I was afraid that if I acknowledged my weakness, others would think my faith was small. I didn't go public about my battle until *after* God rescued me. I am not the only person to hide my areas of weakness.

These days, I proactively confess my weakness and my continuing need for God's help in my fight against panic. Just because I'm healed from one set of fears doesn't mean I should abandon the process. Fear always threatens; panic could take hold from another direction. There may even be hidden layers of fear. So on a weekly basis I press in, ask him to show me anything I'm not seeing.

The need for self-examination never ends. Paul tells us, "Everyone ought to examine themselves before they eat of the bread and drink from the cup."[2] If we do not, he writes, we become sick and weak, bringing judgment upon ourselves.[3] Heart examinations are powerful. I wrestle with my own in the early hours, through prayers and writing in my journal.

The helplessness we feel when we are weak causes us to depend on God for strength and power. This kind of dependence and intimacy is the wellspring of abiding with him. In our utter dependency on God, we learn weakness is nothing to be ashamed of; if we acknowledge it and take it to the Light, it is a tool God uses to expose things we've buried, things he wants to heal in us.

God delights in us. He doesn't want us to live in bondage. When we invite him into our places of weakness, he comes and says, "Let's nail this thing. Let's not dance around it, perform around it, or seek validation to make it feel better. Let's just go after it."

This kind of healing could bring you into one of your richest seasons, but make no mistake about it: when you confess that God is the strength in your weakness, things may seem worse for a time. Why? Because when you find yourself on the cusp of strongholds being released, the enemy marches in double-time.

This is why it is critical to keep declaring the truth: God has promised that when we are dependent on him, he walks with us. Then we can ask whatever we will, and he will lavish us with his power, his goodness, his grace, his kindness, and his mercy. He doesn't want to keep us where we are. When we are brave enough to ask him to meet us in our weakness, he comes. Isn't this encouraging?

Even as I'm writing this book, I'm continuing to learn about power made perfect in weakness. This week I spoke with my dear friend Sarah. At thirty-one, Sarah delivered stillborn twin boys. Exactly one year later, on their birthday, she was wheeled into her first of several cancer surgeries. She's known weakness in ways I can't imagine—five hard years of grief, loss, fear, freedom, and relentless love from the Father. I asked her how she is always so strong. She said there was no other way but to choose the Jesus who sets her free and who never leaves. Sarah has decided to choose Jesus no matter what. That kind of surrender changes us.

Just ask Moses. He's a beautiful picture of surrender in weakness, of needing everything God offers.[4] I love reading about his first encounter with the God of the universe in a burning bush. The dialogue between them makes me laugh because Moses' objections remind me of my own.

> *God:* Go to Pharaoh so you can bring my people out of Egypt.

> *Moses:* What? Who, me?

> *God:* I will be with you.

> *Moses:* What if they ask who sent me?

> *God:* I Am has sent you.

> *Moses:* What if they don't believe me?

> *God:* I'll give you the power to perform signs and wonders in my name.

> *Moses:* But I'm not good with words.

This is where I can imagine God saying slowly and firmly, "Moses, who made your mouth? Go! I'll help you speak, and I'll tell you what to say."[5]

I wonder what God was thinking in that moment. Maybe something like, "Really?! What is it going to take for you to feel confident in the assignment I've given you?"

It's easy to read about Moses' doubt and think, *This is God speaking to you! Don't you trust him?* Then I think of all the times I've determined God must have confused his plans for me with his plans for someone else. I've offered up plenty of, *I can't do this! Just look at my mess!* I wonder what God thinks as he listens to my fears of never-enough-ness.

God does the choosing and assigning, not us. Whew! He calls us, and he equips us. There's no need to run from his calling, to deny it, or wish it away, because "the God of peace, who through the blood of the eternal covenant brought back from the dead our Lord Jesus, that great Shepherd of the sheep," will also "equip [us] with everything good for doing his will."[6]

God demonstrates his power through our frailty. In fact, this is the only thing we can boast in: *His power is made perfect and on full display in our never-enough-ness.* When we are weak, we are actually made strong in Christ Jesus.[7]

Whoa. *The secret to strength is weakness.*

Grasping this has been a game changer for me. I used to think being ill-equipped disqualified me from serving God, but I've learned that when I admit my inadequacy, I invite his power in to strengthen me. This is fertile soil for surrender. Surrender says, *The calling you've laid before me is too great. I cannot fathom it. Still, I will obey. I will trust that you go before me.*

I believe God chose Moses *because* he was weak. God wanted Moses to know he was only able to lead the people because God was with him, giving him everything he needed to do the job.

When you feel weak—or anxious or fearful—the very admission of your weakness could be the moment you realize true strength. And in that moment, you'll see that you are the one God wants to use. You're it. God's glory rests in *you*.

What joy to come before the throne, humbled and low. What freedom to be used, shortcomings and all. This is when we realize that we, *the weak ones*, have been a part of God's plan all along.

The autumn Monday that began with broken words and broken dishes continued to spiral. Darkness lingered as I cried on and off for eight hours, whispering "Jesus" over and over. I went through the motions, drove to the wrong locations at the wrong times for after-school activities. It culminated at 1:30 a.m., when I cried out in the middle of the night from my bed, again and again for Jesus' help.

I can hardly describe the torment I felt: desperation, fear, despair. The words of Paul flashed through my mind: "For our struggle is not against flesh and blood, but against the rulers, against the authorities, against the powers of this dark world and against the spiritual forces of evil in the heavenly realms."[8] What are these powers? They are hidden forces used by the enemy to oppose anyone or anything that is of God.

This freedom journey is serious business, and the enemy *cannot handle it*. He hates the thought that we might live in freedom. The Spirit helped me remember what Paul said to do next.

> "Therefore put on the full armor of God, so that when the day of evil comes, you may be able to stand your ground, and after you have done everything, to stand. Stand firm then, with the belt of truth buckled around your waist, with the breastplate of righteousness in place, and with your feet fitted with the readiness that comes from the gospel of peace. In addition to all this, take up the shield of faith, with which you can extinguish all the flaming arrows of the evil one. Take the helmet of salvation and the sword of the Spirit, which is the word of God."[9]

Clearly, we are supposed to fight the enemy when he attacks us, so that's what I did. I told the enemy to go back to where he came from. I was a child of God, and he had no authority over my heart and mind. I said this out loud, yelled it even (not too loudly since the kids were sleeping), and I was *mad*. I walked upstairs and laid hands on my children as they slept. I whispered prayers for their protection. I sent the enemy away from my house, using Jesus' name.

In those early morning hours, the Spirit met me in my weakness when I confessed, *Save me. Fight for me.* Jesus has done this many times now. Often he had given me the boldness to resist the enemy without too much struggle, to claim the authority we have in the Spirit's power. That night, I asked him to help me claim the authority I have as a daughter to push away the power of darkness.

It worked. The next morning the weight was gone; the kids and I laughed and sang on our way to school. When you resist the enemy, he turns and runs.[10] Sometimes we need to be reminded on the front lines, in our weakness, Jesus is our greatest strength.

Becoming Free

1. Have you been in situations where you felt too weak to fight? What are some examples? Write down ways you want to see God's power made perfect in your weakness.

2. Consider listing the areas of weakness in your life—not to dwell on them, but to offer them up to God as a confession, asking him to take them and transform them into your greatest strength. Journal this to remember. You'll want to be reminded of it in the future.

3. Consider praying this prayer: *Jesus, I name my weakness. Strengthen me as I confess my inability. Show me how your power is made perfect through my weakness.*

12

Free to Celebrate

Expect the end of the world. Laugh.
Laughter is immeasurable. Be joyful
though you have considered all the facts.
WENDELL BERRY[1]

$\mathcal{A}$ FEW FRIENDS ARRIVED at our home just for fun. We gathered around our kitchen island, everyone taking turns at the chips and guacamole. Children belted out karaoke tunes from the playroom upstairs, and we all laughed as Cade performed his one-of-a-kind dance moves nearby. Always up for a captive audience, he began to blow kisses to everyone, followed by a round of hugs. The joy of community was buzzing. Even on the hardest days, life was full of light.

I stood in the corner and watched these good people milling around, laughing. Kids boomeranged each other on the trampoline while Gabe flipped hamburgers on the grill. A smile spread across my cheeks, warming them as joy filled my heart. I was free to celebrate. But it hadn't always been this way.

I'll never forget the day I realized I'd lost my joy.

Somewhere in the clouds over Colorado, our kids were growing restless. The five-hour flight from New York to Salt Lake City required musical chairs. It was Pierce's turn to sit with me, so we decided to watch a slide show on my laptop. Pierce and I huddled together as hundreds of images depicting our family's history rolled across the screen:

Gabe and I as newlyweds

Our first home

My growing tummy

Cade's arrival, so tiny at 4.9 pounds

The wonder in our eyes as new parents

Pierce's arrival

Beloved Pierce in a Steelers jersey being hurled into the air by Gabe in our old backyard

Pierce giggling and tugging on Cade as the two waddled around the room

Finally, the arrival of our third blessing, Kennedy

My shocked and overwhelmed face at Gabe's announcement of "It's a girl!"

Images of pumpkin patches and Halloween costumes and Easter egg hunts and pool parties

Laughter and light had been captured by the camera lens through the years. Time stood still as my son and I took it all in as we flew through the heavens. Suddenly, I saw a single tear stream down Pierce's cheek.

"What is it, son?"

"You seem to have lost your joy since we were little," he said.

The plane might as well have made a nosedive.

"What do you mean, hon?" I asked gently.

As if the knife couldn't go any deeper, Pierce replied, "You don't smile like that anymore."

Was it just me, or was the plane falling toward the ground at breakneck speed?

Then, Pierce's sweet, perfect nine-year-old face crumpled, and I held him as he cried. Dumbfounded, I tried with all my might to hold it together. My sweet, sensitive boy!

"Is it just me, or your dad, too?" I asked.

Pierce confessed that it was both of us. Somehow that didn't help.

I think Pierce's epiphany was as hard for him as it was for me. Time stood still as I seemed to watch my life playing in a rearview mirror. Cautiously seeking to understand, I quietly asked, "When do you think we lost our joy? How long ago?" He thought about it for a while.

"I think about two years ago, or a little more," he said. "When I was around seven."

Three years ago. The year we moved to New York.

I wanted to lock myself in the airplane bathroom and weep, which only reinforced Pierce's point. I'd had no idea my internal struggle was so noticeable. I knew I was pensive, thoughtful, maybe even melancholy at times. But no joy for my children to see? This was too much.

Lord, you could not have staged a more powerful intervention.

I apologized to Pierce, telling him I'd had no idea my life lacked joy, and that I wanted it to be otherwise. I wanted him to see joy on my face and in my actions. I explained that our move to New York had been hard for me, that I was trying my best, but I'd obviously failed him over the last two years in this area and was deeply sorry. On and on I went. Although Pierce felt terrible, and I felt terrible, his unbridled honesty was saving me. *Waking me up.*

Out of the mouth, the heart speaks.[2] I know this all too well. Pierce had spoken from his heart, and now I wondered, *What is my heart speaking?*

In the following moments, everything crystalized. I seemed to see the world through my son's eyes, hear it through his ears. I noticed how my laughter had turned to silence.

The plane landed, and Gabe and I gathered our brood.

As we headed for our rental car, I pondered the words our children heard from me on a daily basis.

"Hurry up!"

"Stop fighting!"

"Clean your room!"

Nagging. Lecturing. The negativity of my own words turned into a pounding gavel in my head. It was like I was hearing for the first time what our kids had been listening to for far too long. When had I stopped nurturing my children?

There had been so much brokenness and pain. I remembered all my meltdowns as I'd tried to hold everything together. What had become of me?

When I had a chance, I stole away to a private place. I paused. Sat still. Listened. Prayed from Psalm 139:

Investigate my life, O God, find out everything about me; Cross-examine and test me, get a clear picture of what I'm about; See for yourself whether I've done anything wrong—then guide me on the road to eternal life.[3]

As I prayed, God revealed to me that my lack of joy sprang from feelings of insecurity—feelings I'd denied out of a desire to appear confident and together. I confessed, *I'm sorry I try to keep up appearances from a place of insecurity. Why do I run so hard when I have already earned your unconditional love? Oh, the pressure! Oh, the joy-robbing sadness of striving. Please restore to me the joy of my salvation.*

Joy—could I even feel it anymore? I'd almost lost hope.

When you live without something for so long, it's hard to remember what it felt like. For all the days I'd lived carefree as a child, I felt like I'd lived an equal measure in a melancholy fog as an adult. Yet I knew the truth—God loved me as I was. He paid the price to set me free, and he longed for me to live in the freedom he secured for me. He wanted me to take joy in my freedom. He wanted me to feel free to celebrate.

A couple of months after my airplane chat with Pierce, I went on a retreat with a small gathering of friends in Austin, Texas. Some I knew better than others, but this was a chance to get reacquainted and dig deeper. The itinerary consisted of long meals, late-night fireside chats, panel discussions, and pool parties.

At the end of the weekend, our host invited us to pray that God would place one of the other women on our hearts, to offer her a word of encouragement, and to pray over her. My friend Shauna walked over to me and as if she could read my heart, put her arm around my shoulders and said, "Joy. I'm praying joy for you in this next season."

A bit embarrassed and a little surprised, I thought, *Is it that obvious?*

God meets us when and where we need it.

A week later, I returned home to a message from another friend who had attended the same retreat. Her name was Joy (of course). Unaware of Shauna's words to me, she said God had impressed on her a simple thought: "Start praying for Rebekah to have joy in her life."

How kind God is! He used his daughters to speak life into my forlorn soul. Those women had no idea how their words breathed hope into my heart. Jesus was about to set me free to rediscover joy—a joy not from within myself, but from him alone.

I wrote in my journal that week:

> *Father, where has my joy gone?*
> *It feels like it slipped down a long drain before I noticed.*
> *How did my labor choke out my laughter? This isn't who I am.*
> *I want to laugh at the days to come.*
> *Help me see what you see; the grins, the jokes, the twinkle in*
>   *their eyes.*
> *Help me behold all that again, in my children and my husband.*

Joy came in the morning, and celebration soon followed.

A few weeks later, I walked through the park on an early spring day with crystal clear skies and tulips practically bursting into bloom. In prayer, I listened and heard God whispering that he'd come "to seek and to save the lost."[4] Something was happening. My confession for a new life, for joy, spurred forward by those unexpected love-reminders from friends, was the perfect storm. Joy was growing in me. What a grace it is, how God brings us back to life.

Eugene Peterson says, "*Salvation* means the healing and rescue of a body that is brought back to the way it was intended."[5] Salvation is not just for our souls; it's for every part of our being, every part of our lives. It is the process of being brought back into a personal, intimate relationship with God, the way it was designed from the beginning. Salvation is a rebirth, a coming alive again.

After I returned home, my attitude began to shift. I started speaking new life into my kids, birthed from this fresh call to live from a place of joy:

"You are my beloved."

"I would give my life for you."

"The things that scare you scare me too."

"We will face those fears together."

"You were meant for amazing things."

"I can't believe I get to be your mom."

"I love your heart."

"I will mess up often."

"I will ask for your forgiveness."

"I will nurture the talents God has planted in you."

Two years after my friends spoke joy over me, our family pulled into a dude ranch near Denver, Colorado, where we were joining several families we'd grown to love. We were a motley crew of denim and boots and wide-eyed grins, the married couples outnumbered by the throng of kids.

After hugs all around, the boys ran off to throw rocks in the creek while the girls went to brush horses in the barn. As the kids dispersed, the mamas gathered around the table inside, starting a hundred conversations and finishing none. We couldn't get our words out fast enough, there was so much life to catch up on as we stuffed our faces with coffee, barbecue, and pie.

Suddenly the kids rushed in, eyes lit up, looking like they were ready to explode.

"Come quick!" they demanded. They had something special to show us, they said, and without a moment to lose. We reluctantly put our conversations on hold and followed them outside. We lifted our eyes to the grandest rainbow I'd ever seen, a complete arc—from one side of the ranch to the other—spanning the sky as far as the eye could see. The kids were convinced we'd find two pots of gold since we could see both ends. Then, as we watched, a second rainbow appeared just above it!

This was celebration. Setting aside the stresses of everyday life, if only for a moment. Bringing the family close. Gazing awestruck at the goodness of God spread across the great western sky.

We began cry-laughing with wonder. We beheld beauty, the promise of God in real time. Words can't describe how majestic it felt. I sensed him smiling down on his daughters, laughing in delight as we in turn delighted in his glory. He reached down to earth, and we received his gift.

The week continued with adventures on horseback—roping cattle, riding trails at sunrise, loping through fields and mountain ridges at sunset. We'd created little nature lovers, Gabe and I. Our kids concocted their own "breakfasts" of bacon, whipped cream, and chocolate chips. We grilled steaks, performed skits, sang on hayrides, and told dating stories under the stars. We created a steer brand with our family name on it, then made our mark on the ceiling in the dining hall.

On the last night, we line danced. Cade took a turn with every pretty girl in the room. He grinned broadly as he twisted and twirled in a round with all our friends smiling and dancing along. I watched him groove to the cadence of his own freedom song, exuding pure joy. Everyone Cade encountered couldn't help but smile in response to him.

Cade's freedom not only allows him to celebrate, but causes others to join in. His joy is contagious. Cade brings life to others. He has taught me what a life of joy looks like. He lights up every room with his unique pronunciation of "Yuh-you" (love you). He passes out hugs like hotcakes. His joy is a grace, a gift of unmerited favor and kindness to everyone he encounters.

Where does joy come from? How does it differ from happiness? What does it mean to truly celebrate?

It took walking through my own wilderness to learn the true source of joy. In the gospel of John, Jesus says, "These things have I spoken to you, that My joy may remain in you, and that your joy may be full."[6]

The joy of Christ becomes our joy.

Mother Teresa put it this way, "When I see someone sad, I always think she is refusing something to Jesus."[7] That's what I did. I carried sadness, depression, anxiety, and fear like a pack on my back.

Jesus says, "Come to me. Bring it. Hand it over. There is nothing I cannot handle. I am more than all the weight you carry. I took it upon myself at the cross."

I took your sin, and gave you righteousness.

I took your tears, and gave you joy.

I took your shame, and gave you forgiveness.

I took your grief, and gave you comfort.

I took your doubt, and gave you hope.

I took your anxiety, and gave you peace.

I took your law, and gave you freedom.

The cross was a switcheroo, and we traded up.

It wasn't the mockery, the whips, the crown of thorns, or the spear that killed Jesus. It took the weight of our sin to crush his heart. He could not die until he'd absorbed it all, every last bit. His words, "It is finished"[8] meant sin was finished. It would hold power over us no longer. Transformation happened in a single moment.

I cannot fathom the kindness of this Jesus—this King of Kings, this Prince of Peace—how he turns all our mourning into dancing, our cries into laughter, our sorrow into joy. Do you see it? Even the Israelites saw it!

When the Lord restored the fortunes of Zion, we were like those who dreamed. Our mouths were filled with laughter, our tongues with songs of joy. Then it was said among the nations, "The LORD has done great things for them." The LORD has done great things for us, and we are filled with joy. Restore our fortunes, LORD, like streams in the Negev. Those who sow with tears will reap with songs of joy. Those who go out weeping, carrying seed to sow, will return with songs of joy, carrying sheaves with them.[9]

This picture of joy after a period of exile offered me hope. I was free to celebrate because God had redeemed my years of lostness, of wilderness, of heartache. Even on the toughest days, I could claim the promise of the cross and resurrection.

Joy is not the absence of darkness. Joy is confidence that the darkness will lift.

The years of sowing in tears, planting the Word of God deep in my heart, gave me a glimpse into a freedom that was only beginning.

Becoming Free

1. Have you walked through a season of something hard? Are you still in the middle of it? Write down what makes it feel so difficult.

2. When is the last time you felt sheer joy? What was it like? What were you doing? Who were you with? Journal about this experience.

3. Do you ever find yourself resisting joy or feeling guilty for experiencing joy? Why? Consider writing out a confession asking God to reveal anything you are withholding from him—any sin, any weight, any burden. Ask him to help you release it, ask him to take it from you and restore the joy of your salvation.

4. Make a list of all the ways God has blessed you. Give joyful thanks for each of these areas of blessing. Celebrate God's goodness!

13

Free to Be Brave

When a more or less ordinary character,
someone who is both kind and self-serving,
somehow finds that place within
where he or she is still capable of courage and goodness,
we get to see something true that we long for.
ANNE LAMOTT[1]

*A*S I WATCHED WOMEN walk into their own freedom stories, I was struck by their bravery. Many were stepping out into the call of God, into the unknown. Many were moving into uncharted waters with God, full of hope and faith.

A sixty-year-old woman told me one spring evening, "For years I've been asking God to *take* my life; tonight I asked him to *save* my life." A fourteen-year-old girl who had just been released from rehab told me God gave her joy to start again.

Countless women—fighting depression, suffering from trauma, treating cancer, holding off divorce, overcoming addictions—were declaring, "I'm done with the life I've created. I want to take Jesus up on what he offers. I want to expect more from a passionate and relentless God. I cannot continue to operate from a place of wounding. I want purpose and freedom."

Humbled by the bravery of these women, by their willingness to confess sin, to seek healing, to walk into their own callings, I considered my own struggle with bravery, how I tripped into it from my earliest days.

I'll never forget my first decision toward bravery, my decision to jump at the end of my elementary years. At the community pool, I climbed to the top of the ladder and walked the plank of the high diving board. As my knees knocked and my toes curled over the edge, I glanced at the deep end below. The ripples felt too far; ten feet was a mighty distance for any nine-year-old. I turned back and descended the ladder, rung after rung, until my bare piggies relaxed on dry ground. For weeks, I tried again. I climbed; I ventured out; I retreated in shame.

What was holding me back?

If grown-up Rebekah could have told nine-year-old Rebekah that the thrill of the release was worth it, she wouldn't have believed it. Letting go couldn't possibly be the point. Instead, I remained enslaved to fear, freedom just beyond my reach. My mom saw my timidity begin to win and quickly enrolled me in a diving class.

Armed with a comrade coaching from below, I felt brave, even invincible. Within a week I closed my eyes and jumped. It was exhilarating. Proud of myself, I scurried up those steps faster a second time and then a third. My diving instructor didn't stop there. The following week he suggested I try a back dive off the high board.

By this point, I was hooked, so I faced backward, heels arched, arms outstretched, and slowly fell back. There was just enough airtime for my body to rotate as my arms raised to cut the water. Just like that, I'd done it.

Each time I surfaced, I squealed a little. My giddy grin couldn't be stopped. My heart pounded with adrenaline each time I climbed the metal ladder, which I did over and over. I began to cheer for the rest of my team, "It's easy! You've got this! Just close your eyes and fall!"

Courage is meant to en-*courage* others.

My triumph on the diving board spilled into other areas of my life. I performed in piano competitions every year starting at age eight. We took music theory, written and auditory tests, all morning, and ended the day with a piano recital where we were judged on a piece played from memory. My hands trembled *every* time. I got used to the knot in my stomach right before going onstage. I'd sit down, smooth my skirt with sweaty palms, place my fingers on the starting keys, and begin.

These are the lessons we learn in our youth: the more we face fear, the braver we become. We see people doing brave things and we think, "If only I had courage like her!"

Fast forward to adulthood.

The first time I ever spoke in public was at a writing workshop, six months before my first book was released. They invited me as a favor to my husband, who was speaking on the main stage. He told them that my story might resonate with the audience, so they added me to the laundry list of breakout sessions. When I stepped up to the microphone, I scanned the eighty people in attendance, and said, verbatim, "This is the first and last time I'll be speaking in public, so here goes." What a great way to begin a talk.

(In hindsight, I don't recommend this.)

I proceeded to cry through my story, sniffling into tissues, ending my time with a rousing offer to pray. I held out little hope of a response. Even my friend Stacy, who had joined me for moral support, sat in the front row, her eyes glued to the ground.

To my surprise, at the end of my session, about fifteen women formed a line to talk. They, too, had been crying. From their comments, I understood that my story had touched them, had offered them something they needed. I'd given language to anxiety and depression, something not often talked about in church. We stayed and prayed for what must have been an hour. My new friends found they were not alone, and a part of each woman's heart came alive. I left hoping to get the chance to speak again, and knew I'd begin differently the next time.

The speaking invitations crept in. While I never intended to speak about the subjects I had written about, saying no would have been an abdication of responsibility. Writing is a solitary sport, something I can do from the safety of my living room sofa while sporting flannel pajama pants. Now, just months after my book was released, I found myself leaving home and flying to new places to speak.

It's worth noting that my first panic attack had occurred when I was on an airplane. Yep, that was the setting. The irony wasn't lost on me as I boarded an airplane each week and buckled myself in to go speak about God's rescue of me. I developed a routine to help calm me: aisle seat, first eight rows if possible to enable a quick exit, relaxing music in my ear buds. No magazines or drama, just my Bible and journal, not because I'm disciplined or spiritual, but because I need truth to envelop me like an airplane blanket. And guess what?

The old place of panic became my sanctuary in the sky.

But airplanes weren't my only barrier to bravery. Speaking itself brought greater fear. At first, I'd write out my talks word for word, only to find myself speaking with my head down, following the script too closely. If I looked up to reference a slide, I'd lose my place in my notes.

A few months into this new vocation, I found myself on another airplane headed to give three forty-five minute talks at a conference. This time, due to weather, my flight was running behind. Stress and anxiety began to creep up. I had only thirty minutes to make my connection in Atlanta's Hartsfield Airport—one of the busiest in the world. I ran from my arrival gate at concourse C, jumped on a train, got off at concourse A, and took the escalator up. Zipping past food stations and SkyMiles promoters, I was the last to board for the final leg of the trip.

As the door of the plane closed and we pushed back from the gate, I had a moment to take a deep breath. As we reached 10,000 feet, I leaned down to get my laptop and put a few finishing touches on my upcoming talks.

My laptop was still in the seat pocket of my last flight.

I arrived at my hotel in a puddle of exhaustion, fear, and frustration. Now what? No notes, no computer for tracking and gathering new thoughts. I tried scratching something out on a pad of hotel notepaper, but there was too much ground to cover. I was at the end of myself.

Falling to my knees, I remembered telling Jesus in my journal one year prior, "If the words become my own, make me mute." Was this his way of getting my attention? I confessed right then:

Never have I wanted my teaching to be about what I bring. I don't want my words to be my own, my talks to be controlled or predictable. But I'm afraid not to plan every word.

I fear I'll be left standing there on stage, lost in thought, staring into space or scratching my head. I'll never feel ready enough, prepared enough, or equipped enough to speak for you.

Will you please help me? Speak through me? Surprise us all with what you have?

God gently responded, *Do you trust me? Do you trust I will give you my words?*

I remembered how God spoke through Isaiah to Israel, "For I am the LORD your God, who stirs up the sea so that its waves roar—the LORD Almighty is his name. I have put my words in your mouth and covered you with the shadow of my hand—I who set the heavens in place, who laid the foundations of the earth, and who say to

Zion, 'You are my people.'"[2] God promised often to put words in our mouths.

After a quick shower to pull myself together, I dressed and arrived at the venue with my Bible and those precious, whispered prayers. I could feel courage starting to form. During our time of worship just prior to my first talk, verses kept flashing through my mind. I remembered reading in John about Jesus saying the Spirit offers us the ability to recall everything he's ever said: "But the Advocate, the Holy Spirit, whom the Father will send in my name, will teach you all things and will remind you of everything I have said to you."[3]

God was looking for this little girl to simply be brave. To not hide behind my notes, my preparation, or my own knowledge, but to walk in faith and be a vessel for him to use. Instead of being constrained by my own words, I would need to be free in order for his words to flow. I'd need to trust that he could do what he said he would do. Sure enough, he showed up.

I taught three sessions without notes that weekend. It was the most free I'd ever felt standing in front of a group of women. We laughed, we cried, we prayed and had the most fun. I was finding a new freedom as I trusted the Spirit to lead me in the moment.

As it turns out, I love telling stories on the fly.

There comes a moment for each of us wherein we must decide—will we be brave, or will we remain enslaved to fear? Will we be brave enough to confess? Will we be brave enough to walk into God's calling? Being brave means no shrinking back or blaming obstacles.

A lifetime of sweaty palms and racing heartbeats has shown me the plain truth:

Bravery is moving scared. Bravery requires stepping out.

The key is to never stop. Nothing may change about our circumstances, but we make a decision. To move. To trust. To be brave.

As I was finding the freedom to be brave, I wanted to make sure the next generation was finding it too. Especially my daughter. I wanted bravery for her and for my future granddaughters. I wanted chains to be broken and liberty to be established. I wanted the freedom to be brave for my entire family.

When my youngest was born, I met my match.

On July 9, 2005, a Saturday morning, Gabe whispered, "It's a *girl*." Seconds passed. Then with complete certainty, Gabe declared, "It's a girl!"

"Can you believe it?" I exclaimed. I was hysterical. During our third pregnancy, we'd decided not to learn our baby's gender. After two boys, I'd given up hope of a girl and wouldn't let myself go there. But there she was, gazing at me with her big blue eyes. My heart could not handle more love at that moment.

I'd tucked the name Kennedy Rose away tight the first moment

I heard it. "Kennedy" felt strong and brave. "Rose" is my middle name, and my mama's, and my mama's mama's, and so on. I was the sixth generation to bear the name "Rose." Choosing an alternate wasn't an option.

Fast forward five years, and this kindergarten blondie was taking New York by storm. With a purse draped over her shoulder and ballet flats over her toes, she skipped along the sidewalks of Manhattan without a care in the world. As the baby girl in any family might do, she boldly asked for anything she wanted, and rarely heard "no" if her Daddy had a say. A few hard and fast lines were drawn, though, and going to bed alone—in her own room—was one of them.

Kennedy couldn't bear to be alone. Most nights she'd sneak into our room or the boys' room. I'd give her a hug and take her back to her bed, then scratch her back and pray while she drifted off to sleep. Those rare times when she was willing to go to bed alone, she'd wake in fear. One night in particular, she was next to impossible to calm, her terror palpable. I wondered if my own panic disorder had affected her.

Fast forward four more years, and Kennedy and I were on a plane to Rwanda. When we arrived our host, Natalie, took us to the Nyamata memorial, one of the worst sites of the Rwandan genocide. We walked across blood-splattered floors to look at the dust-covered piles of clothes of the victims in stacks on benches—baby shoes, toddler shorts, little sundresses. I watched Kennedy take it in; her eyes wide and locked on our guide, she hung on every word. At the end Kennedy signed the guest book with her name, writing, "Thank you for taking good care of the children that died."

My girl was braver than I thought.

Three months later I found her reading *Let's All Be Brave* by Annie Downs. I'd finished tucking in the boys and entered her room to find her beaming from ear to ear. She'd just read Annie's reference to Daniel, how he and three friends stood up to King Nebuchadnezzar by not bowing to his idol. They said *no* when everyone else said *yes*.

I read over her shoulder. "Can you imagine that kind of courage," Annie asked, "to stand when everyone else bows?"[4] They had risked everything, including their lives. Annie pressed further, asking, "Can you say the hard 'no,' knowing it may cost you a lot?"

This challenge was all Kennedy needed to hear; she wanted to serve God with all her heart, no matter what. Kennedy knelt and asked Jesus to take over her life and make her brave. She'd prayed with me at bedtime as a five-year-old in New York City. She wanted Jesus then, because she knew it meant a lot to me. But this time? She wanted salvation for herself.

It's difficult to muster bravery in our everyday lives, isn't it? So often, fear creeps in. *What if I fail? What if others ridicule me?* Our emotions are very real, and I do not wish to minimize them. But God is calling us to step into his plan for our lives with courage, to allow that courage to be a sign to the world that we serve an authority higher than any worldly power. We serve a heavenly king, one who has equipped us for works he's already prepared. Shouldn't that set us free to act with courage and bravery?

Scripture encourages us to have courage when we face difficulty, trials, or fear in our callings. In his letter to the Philippians, Paul wrote, "Whatever happens, conduct yourselves in a manner worthy of the gospel of Christ. Then, whether I come and see you or only hear about you in my absence, I will know that you stand firm in the one Spirit, striving together as one for the faith of the gospel without being frightened in any way by those who oppose you."[5]

Looking back on the ways Kennedy and I both fought to be brave, I take comfort in these words: "'Be not afraid' doesn't mean we cannot have fear."[6] Everyone has fears, but we also have trust and hope and faith.

Our bravest moments come from trusting, from falling into the plan of God. When we do, bravery becomes less about courage and more about faith. We trust God will never leave us or forsake us.[7] We trust everything is possible for those who believe.[8] We trust we can do all things through Christ, who gives us strength.[9] Risk may always feel daunting, but facing fear activates our faith. We'll find ourselves scratching our heads at brave things we can't take credit for, grateful for the One who empowers us.

I want my trust to be louder than my fear, even when I tremble. I want to help others see that fear doesn't have to win. Before we walk into an overwhelming situation, may we set aside an extended time to confess how much we need God's strength and to declare his faithfulness. He is faithful to accomplish whatever he begins and will carry it to completion.[10]

If he is the one who sets this thing in motion, he is the one who completes it.

What a wonderful promise. We are free to be brave. During my journey from airplane panic to telling stories on the fly to rooms full of women, Jesus walked me into freedom. He walks you into freedom too, and the next generation after you. We all have freedom to walk in courage and confidence; we have freedom to be brave. If we want this freedom for our daughters and our granddaughters, we need to pave the way.

Becoming Free

1. What women do you see walking in the freedom of bravery? List their attributes. Do you see similar attributes in yourself, even ones you might be hiding? If so, identify them. Write down three attributes you'd like to grow over the next month.

2. Identify an area or two of your life in which you know there is fear. Are there ways you could engage your fear in baby steps? Little by little? Day by day? List ways you'd like to approach transforming your fear into freedom.

3. What keeps you locked into fear? What are the obstacles that keep you from walking forward bravely? I invite you to write out a prayer of confession of those barriers. Ask God to take them and replace them with his strength and courage.

14

Free to
Love

*If you want to bring happiness to the whole world,
go home and love your family.*
MOTHER TERESA

*T*HERE WAS ALMOST a tender stirring in the crisp winter air of Nashville. It had been eighteen months since our move to this city, since I drove around Franklin nursing my six-week pity party. In spite of my initial resistance, this town had become home.

February brought with it a longing to reestablish myself, to put down roots. We'd bought a home in September. I was inclined to throw a bonfire party for the pile of moving boxes we'd saved and used year after year (five moves to be exact), but settled for recycling them instead.

This year would be one of replanting in a slow and steady way. After seven years of nearly continuous transitions, God was showing me how to root my hope and identity in him. God offered me joy and freedom as I lived into my various roles:

As a wife, *to champion and follow.*

As a mother, *to nurture and raise up.*

As a daughter, *to honor and obey.*

As a friend, *to listen and encourage.*

As a neighbor, *to welcome and nourish.*

As I listened to God, my heart began a gradual shift from wanting to accomplish big things *for* God to wanting to simply receive small things *from* God.

Simple pleasures became significant gifts, such as riding bikes with Cade on his new three-wheeled cruiser or watching our kids run from house to house in our neighborhood with their new friends in tow. Lemonade stands, neighborhood garage sales, campfire cookouts—these treasures were healing my heart, restoring my soul, and bringing me home.

I was overwhelmed, grateful.

It was especially cold that February, with more ice and snow than typical. One Friday morning after the snow finally melted, with the kids back in school, Gabe and I headed out on a "date day." Usually date days meant a long breakfast or lunch, but this time was different.

After a twenty-minute drive into the countryside, we pulled onto a long, winding drive meandering up a flower-laden slope. We'd just celebrated eighteen years of marriage, and in line with our conviction that we needed to put down roots and reestablish ourselves and our relationships, we committed to engage in a few couples' counseling sessions. We'd seen a counselor a handful of times in our married life, usually for a quick fix, a tune-up, or to help us work through a significant disagreement. With the busyness of our life together, there never seemed to be capacity for anything more. But this year we wanted to go deeper in our relationship, to become healthier as individuals and as a couple in order to experience a greater measure of love for each other.

For the first time in a decade, we felt like we could breathe and had time to focus on our marriage. The slower pace of the simple life in Franklin created margin for us to ask new questions, to discern how we could serve each other more, to envision how our marriage might shape the decades to come.

To be fair, I thought we were doing pretty well. I had high hopes for a pat on the back from the counselor. Ninety minutes into the session, it was clear there would be no high fives. As our session came to a close, Gabe said, "Can we add thirty minutes to our session? I think we need to keep this going."

The counselor agreed we should press further. He wanted to dig deeper into our history and explore some areas we'd managed to cover up. So we did.

Gabe and I first met in 1993, at the summer wedding of mutual friends. Although it would be three years before we started dating, our connection was real. From then on, we'd casually bump into each other in our university halls or the cafeteria, at cookouts and birthday parties.

He was the funny and thoughtful guy. I was the entertaining girl always up for a good laugh or a serious conversation. Since we were both in serious relationships during our first years of college, we'd never considered a life together. But over time, as our respective relationships came to an end, we found ourselves reconnecting.

When Gabe and I started spending time together as friends, the potential developed for a dating relationship. I was cautious. Sure, we enjoyed each other, but I couldn't trust my heart. I'd only dated two guys, one in high school and one in college. Both relationships ended painfully. I couldn't bear the thought of another failed relationship, so we tucked the idea of dating away and avoided the topic. If the feelings were there, they would need to wait a good, long while. We decided to put patience to the test.

After months of being "just friends," those close to us began seeing what we had felt all along. Perhaps there could be more. Day by day, we let our guard down. At the end of the summer, we planned a reunion trip with one of our college friends in her hometown of Portland, Oregon. We'd never been to the Pacific Northwest, and with a week free before starting new jobs and real responsibilities, we booked flights.

A city comes alive when you experience it during the early stages of love. Portland's Rose Garden exploded in a sea of color, taking my breath away as we studied (and smelled) the beauty all around us. The vibrant blooms reflected my heart, opening a bit more each day. We hiked Multnomah Falls and ran barefoot on the sand at Cannon Beach, each stunning landscape a jaw-dropping backdrop for another photo op. On our last night, we feasted on salmon and filet mignon at a fancy seafood restaurant overlooking the city. Portland had given us permission to step into what we'd been feeling all along.

As we sat side by side on the flight home, my nerves kicked in. We'd acknowledged a growing attraction toward each other, and as we headed home, we both considered the fact that our relationship would likely become serious. I blamed myself (again) for my previous failed relationships. I harbored a nagging sense that I was always the problem, the one who self-destructed. I was the one whose heart wandered, who couldn't give myself fully to another person. I always withheld a small percentage of my heart, for reasons I couldn't explain.

Am I enough?

Do I deserve a great relationship?

Looking back, I discovered that while I was growing up, I'd felt unknown in some key relationships. As a result, my defenses kicked in when my dating days began. Self-preservation became a cycle of self-destruction. If things didn't work out, I was determined I wouldn't be the one left hurting. My fear of not being enough caused me to run. I didn't know love in its purest form, the way God designed it in the beginning. I couldn't grasp the fullness of being God's beloved.

At the end of our trip, I was at a crossroads with Gabe, afraid I would fail again. In the past, I would stuff down my doubt, ignore it, and keep having fun. *Maybe my feelings will go away,* I always thought. It had never worked before, so this time, I tried something new.

I confessed.

A few days after we returned home to Lynchburg, Gabe could tell I was fidgety and nervous. I was a different girl than I'd been a week earlier in Portland. He told me he was falling in love with me. My heart leapt and then nosedived within seconds. I wanted to hear his declaration of love, but was also deathly afraid of the risk involved. I confessed that I didn't think I'd ever given my heart fully to someone, that I'd held back time and time again in order to protect myself and keep the upper hand.

I finally blurted out, "I don't know how to love."

My words hung in the air. Gabe held me close as tears streamed down my cheeks, and said without batting an eyelash,

"I'm going to teach you how to love."

I don't know what I was expecting, but this was not it. If he was smart, wouldn't he run for the hills? My track record was zero. Yet Gabe seemed unconcerned, almost amused, by my unraveling. His confidence wrapped around me, tethered me. I felt my resistance melt away, replaced by a desire to let him lead the way. Maybe that's what I'd been craving all along, to not have to hold love together, but to collapse into its confident embrace.

A year later I boarded a plane for New York City, ready to surprise Gabe for a weekend. He was there on business (or so I was told), and a friend and I planned a secret visit to surprise him. We hadn't seen each other in almost a month, thanks to his new job in Atlanta.

The joke was on me. He had a grand plan of his own.

I entered my hotel room and found a stunning red dress, suspended as if hanging in thin-air, in the center of the room. There was a note attached with Gabe's greeting, next steps, and tickets to *The Phantom of the Opera*. (I'd told him when we first started dating that one of my dreams was to wear a red dress to *Phantom* on Broadway.)

I embarked on the best makeover a hotel bathroom could offer, zipped up the red dress, and raced to the elevator. I couldn't wait to see Gabe. I thought surely he'd be waiting in the white stretch limo that arrived to pick me up, and I eagerly hopped in. No Gabe. Instead, I found another note that declared his love and told me to press play on the limo's VCR (that's Video Cassette Recorder for those of you born in the digital era). I found myself watching a montage of selected scenes from *An Affair to Remember* and *Sleepless in Seattle*.

You see where this is going, I'm sure. As I watched movie clips of rooftop reunions at the most famous building in Manhattan, the limo pulled up in front of the Empire State Building. I got out of the car alone. An attendant escorted me past the lines of tourists to a private elevator. Eighty-two-year-old Jimmy, the *same* elevator operator who appeared as a teenager in *An Affair to Remember*, escorted me to the 102nd floor. I stepped off the elevator into a round, sun-splashed room of windows overlooking the city. With "Unforgettable" playing in the background and rose petals splattered across the floor, I found my love smiling broadly as he knelt in front of me.

Twenty years later, in a counselor's office on the outskirts of Franklin, we remembered how our post-Portland conversation marked a significant shift in our relationship. I didn't harbor a single doubt for the rest of our dating days about Gabe, about us, or about marriage. I knew his fateful words did not come from his own strength or zeal, but with an assurance that can only come from Christ.

But that day, during our session, I realized I still wasn't completely free to love. Fragments of rejection from the first half of my life still held me captive. I'd brought wounds from past relationships—romantic and familial alike—into my marriage. And when things got stressful or hard, those wounds were exposed. Months after our move to Tennessee, I had to admit my overreactions were affecting our marriage. I wasn't bringing the healthiest version of myself to the equation.

The counselor asked me to explain in more detail, and I proceeded with caution. I explained how when Gabe challenges me, I immediately become defensive. I perceive anything other than praise as criticism or rejection.

I put words in his mouth he never says.

I feel unwarranted shame and want to hide.

I shut down and try to punish him with the silent treatment.

The counselor observed that he had witnessed this firsthand. This was a significant key to our love growing to new levels. He looked me in the eye, and gently but firmly said,

"Rebekah, the goal is to hear something challenging and not break relationship. Running and hiding is an unhealthy response. Staying intimately connected—even when the feedback is not what you want to hear—will be critical to your and Gabe's relationship growth."

This was news to me. Watching the hard truth settle over me, Gabe was quick to mention ways he creates cracks in our relationship as well. But I got the point. I learned a gut-wrenching yet important lesson that day, and I was grateful for it. Even though I'd been a Christian for thirty-five years, there were still areas of my heart that needed to be freed. Once freed, my love for my husband and ultimately others would know no bounds.

In fifth grade I memorized 1 Corinthians 13—the love chapter—but here I was, years later, finally understanding that love truly is the superior way. I was learning that love really is patient.

Love is kind,

Love does not envy,

Love is not boastful, is not conceited.

Love does not act improperly.

Love is not selfish.

Love is not provoked.

Love does not keep a record of wrongs.

Love finds no joy in unrighteousness, but rejoices in the truth.

Love bears all things, believes all things, hopes all things, endures all things. Love never ends.[1]

I re-read this passage after our counseling session that evening, then crawled from my bed, knelt on my carpet, and asked Jesus again,

Where has my love gone? I'm at a loss. I start each day feeling it, but it doesn't take much to send me over the edge. Why do I do this? Why the overreacting? Help me see the root of my wounding. The ways I felt rejected in love. This isn't about Gabe or our marriage. Please pour your love over my heart, like a healing balm. May I come to know your love in such a tangible way that I feel kept by your love, held close by it. Then and only then will I be able to love well from a place of wholeness and healing. Please help me.

I wanted *more* of Christ's love for my husband, our children, and my friends. I wanted freedom from the bondage of anger, unforgiveness, and bitterness—strongholds that were holding me captive, keeping me from loving as Christ loves. I wanted freedom from giving Gabe the silent treatment when we argued, freedom from creating walls when God's love fights to break them down.

It wasn't just Gabe and my family I wanted to love more. *Help me love total strangers,* I prayed. I wanted to love the overlooked, the outcast, and the discarded. I considered all these people and prayed, *Lead me into the freedom to love as you love.*

If love is the superior way, the Jesus way, then surely I couldn't go it alone. Left to myself, I'd stay stuck and unremarkable, loving only what feeds my ego or what builds my worth. The way I see it, we are never too old to ask for a greater measure of love.

As my prayers of confession spilled out, I realized I would never have had the grace to ask for a greater measure of love had I not started relearning and receiving Jesus' love and freedom months prior. As his kindness overtook me, love spilled from his heart into mine. The more I received his love, the more I wanted to love others. Isn't that how everything with Jesus works?

We cannot offer what we do not have.

When I asked Jesus to trade my anxiety for peace, I learned to extend peace to others. When I asked him to restore my joy, I brought laughter to others. Now, I was asking him for a heart consumed by love, a love from Christ that sets prisoners free. Surely he would hear this prayer too. He is gracious to give when we ask.

It's been months since I prayed that prayer, and it is clear that God is leading me into a deeper, more holistic love for Gabe, my family, and the world. He is teaching me to channel his love, to act as a wellspring for those who need it. His love set me free to love.

Maybe you are starved for the freedom that comes from this kind of love. If so, believe this truth:

Everything you've experienced, God was there.

He saw your pain, your joy.

He saw your first steps, your family feuds, your anger and tears.

He saw you when you first went to work, when you got married, when you held your newborn's hand.

He has seen all of your life.

Nothing pushes Jesus away.

Nothing makes him cringe.

He wants you more than life.

He was willing to die in order to make you whole.

Jesus killed sin the day he died; shame has no hold on you.

He knew, before the foundation of the world, that one day you'd hand him every memory of wounding and shame. He takes it all. He was there all along anyway.

Withhold nothing from him ever again.

He will carry you, dance with you, love you infinitely.

Shame is a curse, but forgiveness is life.

Jesus gives life filled up, poured out, spilling over.

He gives life to the full.

Jesus' love will hunt you down until you land on your knees. It knows no bounds; it cannot stop, in spite of all our kicking and screaming. It will lift your head and cradle your heart. It will remind you who you were before all the running. His love will bring you back to life. Jesus set you free to receive his love, and you are free to love others with the same ferocity.

Walk in that freedom.

Becoming Free

1. Are there ways you've been resistant to love? Do you push back against the love of your spouse, your friends, your children, or God? Why?

2. When I asked God to show me how to love more, he revealed to me the sins that were holding my heart captive—sins of anger, unforgiveness, and bitterness—sins I needed to confess. What might you need to confess so that God can set you free to love?

3. Ask God to teach you how to give in to love, how to accept his love and the love of others. Ask him to show you all the people who love you, and all the ways they try to express their love.

4. Pray this prayer: *Jesus, show me all the ways you love me. Teach me to receive this love so that I can accept the love of others. Teach me how to return this love to my husband, my family, and my friends.*

15

Free to Set Free

*Freedom is never voluntarily
given by the oppressor,
it must be demanded by the oppressed.*
MARTIN LUTHER KING[1]

*T*HIS FREEDOM MESSAGE had been brewing for months, although I didn't realize quite where it was heading or how it would land. When you start to experience true freedom and realize it's what God intends, you want everyone to experience it, whether that person is your closest friend or an airplane seat neighbor.

One February morning I boarded a plane. We sat on the snowy runway for what felt like forever, waiting for takeoff, making every effort to beat the storm. After being de-iced three times in three hours, I wasn't sure we would get out. It appeared we might not sleep in our own beds that night.

Suddenly, the woman seated beside the window in my aisle began to have a panic attack. As she gasped for air and pounded her chest, she declared she had to get off the plane. Without thinking, I immediately locked eyes with her and said, "You've got this, girl. I know exactly what you are feeling. I used to suffer from this. I'm not leaving you. If you hang on, I promise it will calm." It wasn't much, but I offered her my Biscoff cookies and pretzels, then called the flight attendant to bring her a drink of Cran-Apple juice mixed with sparkling water. I told her this was my go-to in-flight concoction, and it would make everything better.

I began to ask her questions about herself, where she was going, who she was visiting. We slowly got carried away by conversation, and after a few minutes, she realized she was calm. Hours passed before I considered how natural it felt to help her, to respond involuntarily without overthinking. I marveled at how God blanketed me with an inner calm. It struck me in that moment:

What a gift, to be free to set free.

These things I know:

Freedom begets freedom.

Freedom is contagious.

Freedom helps us set others free.

It's true. Paul wrote that it is for freedom that we have been set free, that we should not carry the yoke of slavery any longer.[2] But Paul didn't stop there. He continues, explaining *how* to live once we are free. "You, my brothers and sisters," he wrote, "were called to be free. But do not use your freedom to indulge [yourselves];; rather, serve one another humbly in love."[3] He takes the guesswork out of freedom.

God wants us to use our freedom for the good of others.

Scripture is full of stories of people who teach and do this very thing. Jude writes that we are to "save others by snatching them from the fire."[4] In the Old Testament, Joshua displays strength and courage as he leads the Israelites from the wilderness and into the Land of Promise.[5] In the New Testament, Paul *takes* life from the church (he killed Christians), then *gave* his life for the church (after his conversion, he spent his life as a missionary of the gospel).[6] All these and many more plain ol' people who became plain ol' heroes of the faith ushered the kingdom of God into their legendary moments in time.

As I've met countless people around the country who were enslaved to various degrees, I've kept asking, *Is kingdom-come freedom really possible today? Can God heal the eighteen-year-old suicide survivor, today? The pastor's wife, who'd been panic-stricken from the age of five, today? The abused and abandoned addict, today? The manic-depressive twenty-something, today? The stage-three breast cancer mama, today?*

Time and time again, God has answered with a resounding "Yes."

When this journey began, I carried all kinds of weight—self-sufficiency and arrogance, guilt and shame. One day I told Jesus I felt like my brokenness was too great. Maybe I'd thwart his plans for my life. Instantly I heard, *What if your purpose is for me to love you?* What could I say to that? No performing, no achievement, no success, and no amount of devoted effort can earn the love of Christ. It is an unconditional healing balm, a freeing balm. It comforted my grieving heart. I knew he was with me, knew me, saw me. It felt like a battle to embrace freedom all over again.

I'm reminded of Joshua and how the Israelites' battles didn't really begin until *after* the Jordan dried up, *after* they left the wilderness, *after* they decided to step into God's promise of freedom, into his Promised Land. No matter the trials and deceptions the enemy would throw my way, I could keep going. Knowing this, when the fears came, I held fast to the words of Paul:

"Don't run back to the yoke of slavery."[7]

Don't run back.

Don't ever run back.

The key has already been found.

The cell door is open.

Run free!

We can write down these words and speak them out loud. We can repeat them to anyone who will listen. We may be tempted to run back, to avoid pain, to hide from rejection, to numb out. But we know the right thing to do: say yes to the Spirit.

I'll never forget one day in the midst of my weakness, I drove down Franklin Road, yelling, "Jesus, you need to get right up in this mess. I'm about to spiral and quit. Please show yourself, now!" To my surprise, he did! The crazy in my brain settled as peace filled my heart and mind.[8] It's true that whoever calls on the name of the Lord shall be saved.[9]

No matter what you've experienced, the pain you've felt, the victimization you've encountered. When God feels far away, *do you see it?*

Confession is the gateway to freedom.

That's it. Every time. This isn't a one-time, "sinner's prayer" kind of thing. This is an Every-Moment-You're-About-to-Lose-Your-Crazy kind of thing. There's no brilliant formula for being a super-Christian. We are all broken and in desperate need of a Savior.

We are *nothing* without him.

We are *everything* in him.

Month by month, Jesus revealed to me what it means to be free. He gently lifted those sins from me as I confessed and released them. I learned the truth of Paul's words in Romans 8: we've been freed from the power of sin, so we shouldn't hold onto it. And it's true—the more I learned to release, the lighter my load became. *Freedom is for those who have nothing else to protect.*

I sought the Lord where he can be found—on the pages of Scripture and on the tablet of my heart. I explored the stories of my past, released shame from decades prior. I rejected the lie that my work made me worthy of love. Confession by confession, I came to know how he sees me, how he loves me, how he sets me free.

Jesus was faithful. He met me in every moment as I wrestled out my freedom, as I recorded it on the page. The confessions you read in each chapter are just a glimpse of the confessions that poured out of me. I cried out for help constantly. Never before had I felt so weak, and consequently, so strong.

There's no boasting here; I brought nothing to this freedom. It was all Jesus.

Three years ago, I asked Jesus to take my heart "back to where it was free and alive and so deliriously joyful it could burst," and that's exactly what he did. I've been set free to confess, to thirst, to ask, to begin again, to step into my calling, to wait, grieve, to be weak, to be brave, to rest, to celebrate, and to love.

Jesus used this story to set me free.

But this isn't just my story. It's yours too. Jesus knew you before you were formed in your mother's womb. He had a purpose for your freedom, even before the beginning of time. He sought you with his everlasting love. Even when you struggle to believe his promises, he'll free you, fill you, heal you, and satisfy your soul. He'll redeem what was broken. Then he'll equip you to tell your story—his story—so that you might set others free. Freedom is never just for the freed. Freedom is a gift that's meant to be shared.

So I ask you, are you learning to walk in freedom?

Do you want to experience the fullness of increasing freedom in your life? What will the result of your freedom be?

Is God calling you to join with him in setting others free?

I believe he is. Do you?

Here's my invitation: be still. Allow God to show you the areas where you aren't free. Confess those areas of bondage. Trust in the promises of God, that he will bring freedom and deliverance.

Let's follow this Jesus together. Let's allow him to take us on a collective freedom journey, shall we? Let's walk with him, arm in arm, and share the stories of the many ways he's set us free. Let's live into the day-by-day adventure of sounding freedom's call. Will you join me?

You are invaluable to the kingdom of heaven. God has appointed a specific role only you can play. You are needed and wanted, chosen and set apart, beloved and worthy. You will receive all power and glory when the Spirit comes upon you. You will bear witness to everything Christ did to set you free.

This is your calling. You are free. Go. Set others free.

Acknowledgments

I can't think of a better ending than to thank the ones who've influenced these words. The plain and simple truth is we need each other, always, to fulfill any assignment God gives us. Without these few, I'd be dead in the water, re-writing the first sentence over and over. Yet they championed and engaged, prodded and questioned, and brought their gifts to the table to inspire mine. We are always better together.

First off, thanks to Carolyn McCready, Seth Haines, and Liz Heaney. You are the champion editorial support group. I'd join you in any ring, any day. You gave this message legs to stand on and pushed me beyond any writing I've ever done. I owe you, always.

To my agent Chris Ferebee, for your encouragement and wisdom; to Dana Tanamachi, for your stunning cover design; to Ann Voskamp, for your dear friendship and gorgeous foreword; you each championed my writing from the beginning, five years ago. I can't thank you enough for believing when this was but a dream.

To generous friends who invested energy into this message: Bob Goff, Korie Roberston, Chris and Lauren Tomlin, Banning Liebseher, Jeff and Alyssa Bethke, Christine Caine, Mike Foster, Jennie Allen, Scott Sauls, Jess Connolly, Adam and Dawntoya Thomason, Havilah Cunnington, Chad Cannon, Katy Boatman, Velvet Kelm, and Courtney Hyder; thank you for always being available to others. You inspire me.

To the loved ones that influenced my stories; Annie Downs, Joy Eggerichs Reed, Shauna Niequist, Sarah Cantrell, Rebekah Witzke, and Lisa Leeman; and to Tom Dean, Brandon Henderson, Robin Barnett, Harmony Harkema, and the rest of the Zondervan team, I shout THANK YOU FROM THE ROOFTOPS for believing in this book. I am deeply grateful.

To friends near and far who watched this story unfold, and cheered loud along the way: Shannon Mescher, Amber Haines, Trina McNeilly, Christy Nockels, Lysa TerKeurst, Tiffini Kilgore, Melissa Zaldivar, Wendy White, Heather Larson, Kathy Bremer, Angie Smith, Raechel Myers, Carrie Allen, and Lori Benham. You are a wild bunch, larger than life in your own unique ways. You taught me to press in when I wanted to quit, because vulnerability is always worth it.

To the Lyons, DeWeese, and Scarberry families, thank you for roots and grounding and permanence. I pray for many more years together, for summers and holidays and memory-making. May I never take our time for granted. Life is as full as we make it.

And finally, to my crew; Gabe, Cade, Pierce, and Kennedy. Whatever the journey, whatever the city, we are together. I've watched your resilience in transition, tenderness in conflict, laughter in love. You make me want to be a better wife and mama. You are my compass, my true north. You've been God's plan for my sanctification. If I never write another word or give another talk, being your wife and mama will always be enough. Everything else is icing. You have my heart, forever.

Notes

INTRODUCTION
1. 1 Peter 2:16–17
2. Galatians 5:1
3. 2 Corinthians 3:17
4. Matthew 6:10
5. Romans 8:11
6. Psalms 14–16
7. Galatians 5:1

CHAPTER 1
1. Anne Lamott, *Bird by Bird: Some Instructions on Writing and Life* (New York: Anchor Books, 1995), 109.
2. Hebrews 12:1

CHAPTER 2
1. Oswald Chambers, *My Utmost for His Highest* (Uhrichsville, Ohio: Barbour, 2000).
2. Psalm 18:6,16,19

CHAPTER 3
1. Frederick Buechner, *Wishful Thinking: A Seeker's ABC* (New York: HarperOne, 1993), 118–119.

2. Viktor Frankl, origin unknown.
3. Psalm 139:13–14
4. Psalm 139:15–16
5. Jeremiah 1:4–9
6. Ephesians 4:1,4–7,11–12
7. 2 Thessalonians 1:11
8. Ephesians 1:11–12
9. Oliver Wendell Holmes, *The Complete Works of Oliver Wendell Holmes* (Boston: Houghton-Mifflin, 1909), 247.

CHAPTER 4

1. Parker J. Palmer, *Let Your Life Speak: Listening for the Voice of Vocation* (San Francisco: Jossey-Bass, 2000), 33.
2. From Ann's keynote address at the 2013 Allume Conference, http://allume.com/2013-keynote-videos/
3. James 5:16
4. *Cambridge Dictionary of American English* (Cambridge University Press, 2007).
5. From the New King James Version
6. Romans 8:2
7. Romans 8:17; Galatians 4:4–5
8. Titus 3:4–7
9. Hebrews 12:29
10. Romans 8:38–39
11. Galatians 5:1
12. 1 Corinthians 6:20; Galatians 3:13
13. Psalm 126:6

CHAPTER 5

1. Jerry Bridges and Bob Bevington, *The Bookends of the Christian Life* (Wheaton, IL: Crossway, 2009), 61.
2. Matthew 11:30
3. Amos 8:11
4. Exodus 17:1–3

5. Exodus 17:5–7

6. Joshua 3:8 NLT

7. Joshua 3:13

8. Matthew 14:13–21

9. Ephesians 3:20

10. John 6:35–36,40 (emphasis mine)

11. John 19:28

12. John 4:1–34, (paraphrased)

13. John 4:29

CHAPTER 6

1. Dwight Lyman Moody, *Prevailing Prayer: What Hinders It* (New York: F.H. Revell, 1885), 90.

2. Luke 9:13

3. Origin unknown

4. James 5:13–18

5. Luke 22:42

6. Matthew 17:20, Luke 17:6

7. 2 Corinthians 12:7

8. Matthew 18:19

9. Mark 11:24

10. Luke 11:10

11. John 14:13

CHAPTER 7

1. Wendell Berry, *The Mad Farmer Poems* (New York: Counterpoint, 2008), 13.

2. Proverbs 22:6

3. Psalm 127:4–5 (paraphrased)

4. Psalm 139:1–3,7–10

5. John 14:23

CHAPTER 8

1. Fulton J. Sheen, *Life of Christ* (New York: McGraw-Hill, 1958).

2. Psalm 23:1 KJV

3. 1 Corinthians 1:4–5,7

4. Ephesians 3:20 NKJV

5. Galatians 6:9

6. Hebrews 10:35–36 NKJV

7. Psalm 13:1

8. See Psalm 91:4

CHAPTER 9

1. C. H. Spurgeon, *Lectures to My Students: a Selection from Addresses Delivered to the Students of the Pastors' College, Metropolitan Tabernacle, London* (New York: R. Carter & Bros., 1890), 260.

2. Julia Cameron, *The Artist's Way* (Los Angeles, CA: Jeremy P. Tarcher/ Perigee, 2001), 1.

3. Matthew 11:28–30 MSG

4. Isaiah 30:21

5. Andrew Murray, *Abiding in Christ* (Minneapolis, MN: Bethany House, 2003), 25.

6. Phil. 3:12

7. 2 Peter 1:3

8. Andrew Murray, *Abiding in Christ* (Minneapolis, MN: Bethany House, 2003), 30.

CHAPTER 10

1. Parker J. Palmer, *Let Your Life Speak: Listening for the Voice of Vocation* (San Francisco: Jossey-Bass, 2000), 58.

2. This wisdom was shared with Gabe by a counselor named Al Andrews.

3. Matthew 5:4

4. John 11:33–35

5. Colin Brown, ed. *Dictionary of New Testament Theology,* vol. 2 (Grand Rapids: Zondervan, 1976), 416–417.

6. Luke 19:41–22

7. Colin Brown, ed. *Dictionary of New Testament Theology,* vol. 2 (Grand Rapids: Zondervan, 1976), 417–419.
8. Matthew 26:37–38 NLT
9. Romans 8:26, BSB
10. Richard Rohr, *Falling Upward: A Spirituality for the Two Halves of Life* (San Francisco: Jossey-Bass, 2011).

CHAPTER 11

1. 2 Timothy 1:7 NKJV
2. 1 Corinthians 11:28
3. 1 Corinthians 11:30-32
4. See Exodus 3:10–14
5. See Exodus 4:1–13
6. Hebrews 13:20–21
7. 2 Corinthians 12:9–10
8. Ephesians 6:12
9. Ephesians 6:13–17
10. James 4:7

CHAPTER 12

1. Wendell Berry, *The Mad Farmer Poems* (New York: Counterpoint, 2008), 13.
2. Luke 6:45
3. Psalm 139: 23–24 MSG
4. Luke 19:10
5. From a lecture Eugene Peterson gave to a group of Q attendees in New York City, 2011.
6. John 15:11 NKJV
7. Mother Teresa, *Come Be My Light: The Private Writings of the Saint of Calcutta* (New York, NY: Doubleday, 2007), 33.
8. John 19:30
9. Psalm 126

CHAPTER 13

1. Anne Lamott, *Bird by Bird: Some Thoughts on Writing and Life* (New York: Random House, 1994).
2. Isaiah 51:15–16
3. John 14:26
4. Annie Downs, *Let's All Be Brave* (Grand Rapids, MI: Zondervan, 2014), 115.
5. Philippians 1:27–28
6. Parker Palmer, *Let Your Life Speak: Listening for the Voice of Vocation* (San Francisco: Jossey-Bass, 1999), 93.
7. Deuteronomy 31:6
8. Mark 9:23
9. Philippians 4:13
10. Philippians 1:6

CHAPTER 14

1. 1 Corinthians 13:1–8 (paraphrased)

CHAPTER 15

1. Martin Luther King, Jr. "Letter from a Birmingham Jail." *African Studies Center*. University of Pennsylvania, Web.
2. Galatians 5:1
3. Galatians 5:13
4. Jude 1:23
5. Joshua 1–5
6. Galatians 1
7. Galatians 5:1 (paraphrased)
8. Philippians 4:7
9. Joel 2:32; Acts 2:21; Romans 10:13

RHYTHMS OF RENEWAL

Trading Stress and Anxiety for a Life of Peace and Purpose

DISCOVER HOW TO:

- Take charge of your emotional health & invite others to do the same.
- Overcome anxiety with daily habits that strengthen you mentally.
- Find joy through restored realtionships in your family & community.
- Walk in confidence with the unique gifts you have to offer the world.

Available in stores and online!